Published in 2020 by Welbeck
An imprint of Welbeck Publishing Group
20 Mortimer Street
London W1T 3JW

A CIP catalogue record for this book is available from the
British Library

ISBN 978-1-78739-369-1

Printed in Dubai

10 9 8 7 6 5 4 3 2 1

CONTENTS

Imogen

march 2020

INTRODUCTION

Means, motive and opportunity: this isn't just the method by which any criminal investigation is conducted.

Establishing the tools with which the crime was committed, what the actionable idea behind the crime was and when the chance to commit the crime occurred can help define the criminal. Where the three points of this Venn diagram of murder converge, there lies a window into the mind of a serial killer, a glimpse of an often chaotic, disturbed and disturbing psyche.

Serial Killer profiles a broad spectrum of deadly murderers by this method, some of whom will be familiar names, as their crimes have gained notoriety through the true crime genre and fictionalized accounts of their horrendous acts. By viewing these criminals through the more objective lens of the categorical trinity of means, motive and opportunity, this book will give you a better understanding of who these people really were, what drove them to kill and whether their crimes were inevitable. In short, if they were born to kill.

Ben Biggs

3. R. MIDDLE

CROWN PRINCE SADO

Born Prince Jangheon to King Yeongjo of dynastic Korea, though he was posthumously named "Sado" by his father. Sado was a deeply paranoid and disturbed man who regularly beat and murdered his cowering servants for the slightest perceived error.

MEANS

He used his bare hands and heavy household objects to beat his victims. On one occasion, he used a knife to sever the head of a servant who had failed him and paraded it around the palace, showing it to his horrified wife and her servants.

MOTIVE

Sado was likely to be the next in line to the throne but his father refused to give him any authority over his kingdom, probably because he felt he was unfit for command. He would humiliate Sado in public and in front of the servants, which meant Sado formed closer bonds with the women in his family. When his sister, grandmother and mother all died within a relatively short space of time, Sado's weak grip on sanity finally slipped. He once told his wife, "It relieves my pent-up anger to kill people or animals when I am feeling depressed or on edge."

OPPORTUNITY

He became obsessive about clothing and his dressing routine. He made his staff lay dozens of outfits out for him daily, selecting some to burn as an offering to "ghosts". When he settled on something to wear, his eunuch servants would pray that nothing would go wrong.

CAPTURE

When Sado threatened his own father, his fate was sealed. King Yeongjo ordered him to climb into a rice chest on a hot day and was left inside for a week until he died.

**1735–1762
LOCATION: KOREA
YEARS ACTIVE:
1757–1762
MURDERS: 3+**

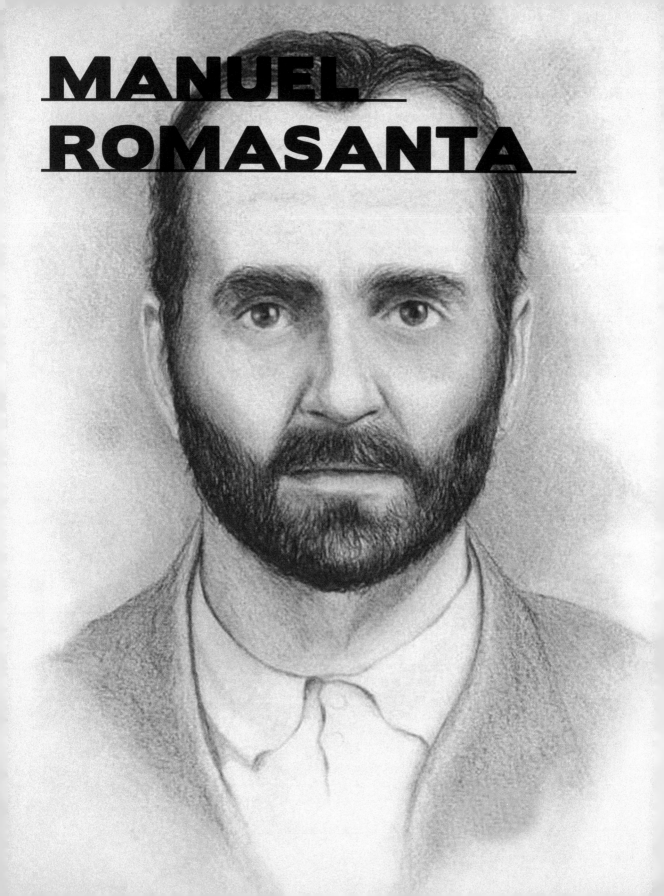

MANUEL ROMASANTA

Spain's first recorded serial killer was known as the "Werewolf" not because of the gruesome manner in which his victims – all women and children – died, but because Romasanta claimed to be suffering from "lycanthropy" (a mythical disease that turns a man into a wolf) as his defence.

MEANS

Details of exactly how Romasanta killed his victims have not been recorded, but he was a small man (under five feet tall) and might have lacked the strength to overpower a grown woman. He butchered his victims with a knife, so it's likely that he stabbed them to death first.

MOTIVE

Some experts have put forward the theory that Romasanta was intersex – possessing both male and female sexual organs – based on his small stature and the fact that his parents thought he was a girl up until the age of six. The confusing nature of this condition and his upbringing could have affected his behaviour. Many now believe that he suffered from antisocial personality disorder.

OPPORTUNITY

He was a tailor, and claimed to have contacts with wealthy clients who had places for women and their children in their houses. His victims, from towns in northern Spain, would leave with Romasanta and never return. Romasanta would then sell their clothing and possessions.

CAPTURE

After families in Escalona became suspicious of Romasanta, who was selling the clothing of the missing women, he was arrested.

SENTENCING

Romasanta was convicted of nine murders and sentenced to death in 1854. This was commuted to life imprisonment after a French hypnotist asked the court permission to study him. Romasanta died in prison under mysterious circumstances a few months later.

**1809–1863
LOCATION: SPAIN
ALSO KNOWN AS:
"THE WEREWOLF
OF ALLARIZ"
YEARS ACTIVE:
1843–1851
MURDERS: 9+**

AMELIA ELIZABETH DYER

Victorian baby farmer Dyer killed over a dozen children across Southern England purely in the name of financial gain.

MEANS

The heartless Dyer thoroughly deserved the moniker "The Ogress of Reading". She took advantage of the vulnerable system of "baby farming" – the Victorian practice of charging a fee to take care of unwanted and illegitimate young children – and exploited it to the extreme. She advertised her services and then, when she had the money from an unsuspecting parent (often a single, impoverished mother), the baby that had been deposited in her care was simply strangled and dumped into the River Thames.

MOTIVE

Greed played a pivotal part in the murders: by killing the babies, Dyer saved herself a lot of money, time and effort taking care of the child's basic needs. It also meant she could adopt more children and continue profiting. It's likely that she suffered from mental-health issues, though she was a cunning woman who knew how to feign insanity to avoid the hangman's noose.

OPPORTUNITY

To avoid suspicion, she would frequently relocate to other parts of England where she wasn't known. Her adverts invariably popped

up wherever she settled, including in the *Bristol Times & Mirror* a few months before she was arrested.

CAPTURE

Dyer was arrested in April 1896 and charged with murdering 12 babies, though she is likely to have killed dozens, if not hundreds, more.

SENTENCING

Victorian justice finally caught up with her in June 1896, when she was executed at the infamous Newgate Prison in London.

**1836–1896
LOCATION: UK
ALSO KNOWN AS:
"THE OGRESS OF READING"
DATES ACTIVE: 1880–96
MURDERS: 12+**

THE BENDER FAMILY

This US frontier "family" (historians suspect they might not have been related) had an elaborate system of murdering and robbing weary travellers who stopped at their trailside home.

MEANS

In post-Civil War America, the four members of the alleged Bender family – parents Elvira and John, daughter Kate and son John Jr – set up a homestead next to the Great Osage Trail in Oklahoma. Here, the Benders had constructed a crude but effective killing method in which they all played a role. Kate was an attractive woman and would lure men into their house. They would be given the seat of honour for a meal in front of a wagon canvas that had been hung to cover the back room. When the moment was right, John would spring out from behind the canvas and strike them with a claw hammer, while Elvira, Kate or John Jr would cut their throats with a small blade. The victim's seat was positioned over a trap door that led to the cellar, where they would be thrown to die. The bodies wound up fertilizing the Benders' vegetable patch.

MOTIVE

The Benders were driven by greed: large sums of cash, horses and valuable items were stolen from the people they murdered – travellers looking to start a new life west of the frontier or traders heading back east. Once the unfortunate victim dropped into the cellar, they were stripped of everything. There is circumstantial evidence that the Benders also enjoyed the kill in and of itself, as some of their victims didn't have anything of value on them that would have made it worth a murderous bandit's time.

OPPORTUNITY

As a waypoint in the prairie wilderness, the little house must have seemed like a lifeline for weary travellers looking for a roof over their heads and a hot meal, but victims walked right into the trap. A few wary guests who survived their encounter with the Benders reported noticing suspicious stains on the canvas, or seeing a hammer being secreted by John.

CAPTURE

Despite the authorities tracing the source of the disappearances along the trail to the Bender property, where numerous bodies were found, all four of the Benders managed to escape and never faced a court.

1800s (ESTIMATE)
USA
ALSO KNOWN AS:
"THE BLOODY BENDERS"
MURDERS: 12+ (ESTIMATE)

H.H. HOLMES

This nineteenth-century Chicago killer is best known for the elaborate hotel he build to facilitate his murders.

MEANS

By the time Holmes had finished building his "murder hotel", an expansive three-storey building in the Englewood neighbourhood of Chicago, he'd already had some experience with insurance scams and quite probably murder, too. He had constructed a maze of hidden murder chambers and passageways into the hotel, complete with soundproofed rooms and a chute where you could slide bodies directly into the basement. Vats of acid and quicklime, obtained via his ground-floor pharmacy, would make short work of his victims' remains. Holmes was a smart and charming psychopath who held down three marriages, in different cities, to wives who knew nothing of each other's existence. Winning the trust of both men and women came easily to him.

MOTIVE

Holmes's true character has been obfuscated by the pulp fiction of the 1940s, which portrayed him as a maniac guesthouse owner who devised an elaborate way to extort money from his victims. He certainly robbed the people and then claimed on the insurance policies he'd levy on his guests. But Holmes revelled in the power he could exert over the people who submitted themselves to being a guest at his "murder hotel". The thrill of rape, torture and murder was at least as compelling as the profit he could make from engineering their deaths.

OPPORTUNITY

Once his "World's Fair Hotel" had been set up, he didn't need to actively prospect for victims. One of his first known murders was that of Julia Smythe, the wife of an employee in his pharmacy, and her daughter, Pearl. After Smythe's husband moved away following his discovery of her affair with Holmes, mother and daughter disappeared on Christmas Eve 1891. Minnie Williams, whom Holmes employed as his stenographer, disappeared under similar circumstances along with her sister Nannie – but only after she had signed the deed to a property she owned in Fort Worth, Texas, over to a mysterious third party.

CAPTURE

He was arrested in 1894 and held on an outstanding warrant from Texas for horse theft, before authorities charged him with the murder of his accomplice and right-hand man Benjamin Pitezel, in 1895. After his conviction, Holmes confessed to 27 murders.

SENTENCING

Holmes was found guilty of murder and sentenced to death by hanging.

1861–1896
LOCATION: USA
YEARS ACTIVE: 1891–94
MURDERS: 9+

ALBERT FISH

Child-eating killer Albert Fish taunted the parents of one of his victims, sending a letter that described how the girl tasted.

Fish was a painter and decorator at one point, giving him access to the homes of unwitting families, and he was a practised liar, which allowed him to pull the wool over the eyes of potential victims and their parents. Many of his young victims were African Americans, orphans or the mentally disabled – individuals who had fallen into the gutters of nineteenth-century New York society and whom Fish assumed would not be missed. Under his mattress, Fish kept a murder kit consisting of a cleaver, knife and handsaw, which he'd dubbed his "implements of hell".

MOTIVE

Fish's family had a history of mental illness: his parents and many of his siblings and relatives suffered from diagnosed psychoses or addictions of one description or another. His deviant sexual interests developed at an early age, and after his mother gave him away to an orphanage, Fish discovered great pleasure in being whipped as well as inflicting pain on others. He once remarked that he "always seemed to enjoy everything that hurt". As the years passed, Fish developed a taste for raw meat, which he sometimes served to his own family on Sundays.

OPPORTUNITY

One of the best-documented cases of Fish's crimes was that of 10-year-old Grace Budd. He'd told her parents that he was a local farmer who was hosting a party for his niece, who was the same age as Budd, and convinced them to let him take her to the venue. Grace Budd was never seen again. Seven years later, after another man was convicted of her murder, Fish wrote to the Budds, describing in stone-cold detail how he strangled, dismembered, cooked and ate her.

CAPTURE

The letter to the Budds proved his undoing. It was traced to Fish and he was finally tried for her murder, and that of two others, in 1935.

SENTENCING

Fish never denied the murders. He was found to be sane and was sentenced to death by electric chair, the prospect of which he described as "the supreme thrill of my life."

**1870–1936
LOCATION: USA
YEARS ACTIVE:
1924–34
MURDERS: 3+**

PETER
KÜRTEN

Kürten was a particularly savage killer, mostly of women in and around Düsseldorf, who sometimes drank from the bleeding wounds of his victims.

MEANS

He often used knives, scissors or sharp implements to stab his victims and inflict multiple wounds. He also manually strangled and used a hammer to kill several of his victims. He doused the body of one of his victims in kerosene and set her alight.

MOTIVE

Kürten was physically abused by his father when he was young and after that, began to commit small acts of arson and petty theft – and even drowned two of his school friends (it was officially ruled an accident). At age 13, Kürten discovered that he could achieve a much greater sense of sexual satisfaction by having sex with farmyard animals and stabbing them just prior to climax.

OPPORTUNITY

Most of his victims were selected completely at random, and others were dragged off as they passed him on the street. Maria Hahn was killed after Kürten arranged a date with her, and then lured her into a field. In his first known murder, that of nine-year-old Christine Klein, the victim was murdered in her own bed after Kürten broke in to steal from her room.

CAPTURE

After numerous witness accounts and a huge police investigation, Kürten told his wife about his double life in 1930 and urged her to hand him in for the reward.

SENTENCING

He was sentenced to death and executed by guillotine.

1883–1931
LOCATION: GERMANY
ALSO KNOWN AS: "THE VAMPIRE OF DÜSSELDORF"
YEARS ACTIVE: 1913–1929
MURDERS: 9+

LEONARDA CIANCIULLI

Cianciulli murdered three women in Corregio, northern Italy, but became infamous in her home nation for what she did with her victims' bodies.

MEANS

She would drug her victims with wine laced with sedatives, then kill them with an axe. Cianciulli knew how to render fat into soap and kept an iron pot nearby, into which she would drop the dismembered body parts before boiling them in a caustic soda solution. She would then render the fat into soap and also biscuits, which she would supply to her neighbours.

MOTIVE

Ten of Cianciulli's children had died young and this had an undeniable effect on her mental health. In 1939, when she discovered that her eldest son Giuseppe had joined the army to fight for Italy in World War II, she despaired. She decided that she could protect him by sacrificing a human – and while she was at it, con her victims out of their life savings.

OPPORTUNITY

Three of Cianciulli's neighbours fell foul of her macabre plan. Faustina Setti, Francesca Soavi and Virginia Cacioppo were invited over to her house under the pretence that she had secured them a good job, or in Setti's case, found her a suitable partner, in distant towns. They had paid her handsome sums of money for this service. Cianciulli had cunningly convinced each of them to tell no one of their move and to write letters addressed to friends and relatives telling them in advance that all was well, ready to be mailed when they reached their destination.

CAPTURE

Police eventually began to suspect Cianciulli's son, Giuseppe, of being involved in Cacioppo's disappearance. Ever protective of her remaining children, Cianciulli immediately confessed to the murders.

SENTENCING

In 1946, Cianciulli was sentenced to 30 years in prison plus three in a criminal asylum, but died shortly before she was due to be released.

**1894–1970
LOCATION: ITALY
ALSO KNOWN AS:
"THE SOAP-MAKER
OF CORREGIO"
YEARS ACTIVE:
1939–1940
MURDERS: 3**

MARCEL
PETIOT

This French doctor exploited the Nazi persecution of Jews, setting up a phony escape route in the basement of his Parisian property and charging refugees a fortune for safe passage out of occupied France, before killing them and stealing their possessions.

MEANS

Petiot owned a house on rue le Sueur in Paris, the basement of which he set up for the disposal of bodies using a quicklime bath and coal-fired stove. He had access to cyanide, which he administered to his victims in lethal doses.

MOTIVE

For an intelligent man with no moral scruples and a mind for criminal enterprise, Petiot must have quickly realized the financial opportunity that the occupation of Paris afforded him. He saw how desperate Jewish families fleeing the Nazis were and how no one would miss them if they disappeared, the assumption being that they had escaped, were in hiding or had been transported by the Nazis.

OPPORTUNITY

He had already established a reputation for himself as a doctor willing to prescribe narcotics, provide medical certificates for fake illness and otherwise use his authority as a general medical practitioner to circumvent the law – for a substantial fee, of course. He would charge Jewish families 25,000 francs to flee to South America via his escape network. On the appointed day, they would turn up at Petiot's house with everything they owned. The doctor would tell them he needed to vaccinate them against disease on their long journey ahead, and then inject them with deadly poison.

CAPTURE

Though the Gestapo investigated Petiot for assisting Jews in escaping France, it wasn't until the Nazis had been forced out of Paris that Petiot was arrested, after neighbours complained about the foul smell coming from his property. Bones and charred remains were found in his basement.

SENTENCING

Petiot was convicted of murdering 27 people, though suspected of many more. He was beheaded on 25 May 1946.

**1897–1946
LOCATION: FRANCE
YEARS ACTIVE:
1942–1945
MURDERS: 27+**

ZSUZSANNA FAZEKAS

In the early twentieth century, a midwife living in the village of Nagyrév in central Hungary began to supply the women who came to her with poison, encouraging them to kill their husbands. She and 26 others became known as "The Angel Makers of Nagyrév".

MEANS

Fazekas herself had some basic medical training and knew how to distil arsenic from flypaper simply by soaking it in water, which she encouraged some of her patients to do.

MOTIVE

Hungarian society at the time was extremely conservative, and divorce was strictly forbidden, even if the husbands were violent or gave themselves up to alcohol too frequently. When the men were drafted into the army at the outbreak of World War I, some of the wives had affairs with Russian prisoners of war who were brought in to work on the land. When their husbands returned, the wives wanted to be rid of them. Giving them the means and method to murder gave Fazekas status and earned her a few coins, too.

OPPORTUNITY

Even before the war, the women came to Fazekas with their medical complaints, as there was no doctor in the village. While there they would invariably complain about their husbands. At which point Fazekas would either give them some arsenic or share the flypaper method of making it, telling them it was a "simple solution" for their problem.

CAPTURE

As the village menfolk dropped dead over the years, police became suspicious. Acting on some dark rumours, they exhumed 50 bodies, 46 of which were found to contain arsenic. The authorities then moved in to arrest Fazekas.

SENTENCING

Fazekas committed suicide before she could be arrested, but 26 of the accused women went to trial. Of the 26, eight received the death sentence and the rest went to prison, seven of them for life.

**UNKNOWN–1929
LOCATION: HUNGARY
YEARS ACTIVE:
1911–1929
MURDERS: UP TO 300**

NANNIE DOSS

Born in Blue Mountain, Alabama, Doss systematically killed family members and husbands throughout her life before her arrest at the age of 49.

MEANS

Poison was Doss's weapon of choice, including rat poison on at least one occasion.

MOTIVE

Over the course of several decades, Doss wiped out a large part of her family, including four husbands, her sister, grandson, and her mother-in-law, though two of her children and a granddaughter could likely also be counted among her victims. In most of the murders, she claimed reasonable sums of insurance money. Doss herself said in a prison interview that money had nothing to do with the murders and that she killed her husbands in search of "the perfect mate". A serious head injury when she was younger, after which she suffered headaches and blackouts for years, could have contributed to her behaviour and lack of impulse control.

OPPORTUNITY

Her first husband, Charles Braggs, claimed to have been "scared" and suspicious of Doss after two of their four children died of "food poisoning" on separate occasions after he left for work. Braggs managed to extricate himself from their relationship without becoming one of her victims. Doss's daughter Florine left her son Lee with Doss for a few days and he died under similar circumstances, while both of Doss's sisters collapsed and died while she was visiting them.

CAPTURE

An autopsy of Doss's fifth husband, Samuel Doss, finally revealed that he'd ingested enough arsenic to kill 20 men. When police confronted her with their suspicions and this evidence, she confessed.

SENTENCING

Doss was given a life term in 1955, but died of leukaemia 10 years later.

**1905–1965
LOCATION: USA
DATES ACTIVE:
1920s–54
MURDERS: 11**

ED GEIN

The reclusive Gein was a grave robber, who took trophies from the corpses he exhumed from the cemetery in his hometown of Plainfield, Wisconsin. He killed two women and fashioned their body parts into macabre items of clothing and household objects. He is a murder suspect in the deaths of several others, including his own brother.

MEANS

Gein shot both his live victims, Mary Hogan and Bernice Worden, with a hunting rifle. He used a truck to transport their bodies to his house, where he lived alone after his mother died. He trussed the dead women up like deer on a wooden crossbar in his shed, butchering them with knives and tanning their skin and body parts.

MOTIVE

Gein's mental state had been questioned long before he was arrested for murder and the gruesome contents of his house were discovered. His mother was his only friend and, in a way, a mental anchor for Gein. When she died in 1945, he drifted into despair and self-loathing. He sought ways to recreate her and claimed to have frequently "blacked out" when he found himself at Plainfield's cemetery. He had a similar blackout around the time of Bernice Worden's murder.

OPPORTUNITY

Bernice Worden's hardware store was closed on 16 November 1957, to the disappointment of her customers. Her son entered at 5pm that evening to discover blood stains on the floor, the cash register open and a sales receipt from the last customer that morning – Ed Gein.

CAPTURE

Gein was arrested shortly after the sales receipt was discovered, his house searched and the remains of both Bernice Worden and Mary Hogan discovered. He confessed to both murders.

SENTENCING

At his trial, he pleaded not guilty by reason of insanity and was declared unfit to stand trial. He was committed to the Central State Hospital for the Criminally Insane in Wisconsin, where he was diagnosed with schizophrenia.

**1906–1984
LOCATION: USA
ALSO KNOWN AS:
"THE BUTCHER OF
PLAINFIELD"
YEARS ACTIVE:
1954–1957
MURDERS: 2+**

EDWARD LEONSKI

Leonski was an American soldier posted to Camp Pell in Melbourne during World War II. He became known as the "Brownout Strangler" because he killed his victims at a time when "brownouts" (dimmed lighting, as opposed to Europe's wartime blackouts) were mandatory in Melbourne.

MEANS

He was a young and strong man, a boxer and bodybuilder who was easily capable of killing the women he preyed upon with his bare hands.

MOTIVE

His family in New Jersey had a history of mental illness and he had an intensely controlling mother. He was also an alcoholic and a nasty drunk, who would pick fights at bars when he wasn't lining up his next victim. He'd already learned that it was possible to get away with assaulting women after an attack on a woman in San Antonio, Texas, went completely unanswered by the courts. Leonski never had any kind of meaningful relationship with anyone, man or woman, and the psychologist who interviewed him for the trial reported that his murders were born out of a symbolic revenge against his mother.

OPPORTUNITY

Leonski could be charming when he needed to be. Two of the three women he would go on to kill, Ivy McLeod and Pauline Thompson, met him under ostensibly romantic circumstances. To the chagrin of Australian men, American troops in uniform had the advantage when it came to the pursuit of local women at the time. Unfortunately for McLeod and Thompson, whose bodies were arranged in degrading positions after death, their boyish, smiling date turned out to be a monster.

CAPTURE

Leonski, drunk as he was each time he killed, wasn't careful. Witnesses had spotted the American soldier with one of the victims, and he was fingered in a line-up.

SENTENCING

US General Douglas MacArthur, keen to limit the damage to the US Army's image, made sure Leonski felt the full force of a military court martial. Leonski was executed by hanging.

**1917–1942
LOCATION: AUSTRALIA
ALSO KNOWN AS:
"THE BROWNOUT
STRANGLER"
YEARS ACTIVE: 1942
MURDERS: 3**

ARCHIBALD HALL

English killer Hall worked his way into the employment of wealthy aristocrats, where he hatched elaborate plots to obtain their wealth.

MEANS

Subsequently known by several monikers including the "Killer Butler", Hall was an intelligent criminal, a thief who graduated to burglary, before studying antiques and aristocratic etiquette in prison to further his murky profession. He became a butler to a wealthy Scottish dowager, Margaret Hudson, when he was in his fifties, but soon decided he liked his job and employer and he would "go straight" – a resolution that didn't last long. In his new cover career, Hall had access to shotguns, fire irons and the trappings of wealthy life. He would later use these items to overpower and kill his victims.

MOTIVE

The five murders themselves were a means to an end: that of silencing the people Hall thought might shop him to the police for stealing from his employers, and inevitably put him behind bars again.

OPPORTUNITY

His first known murder was gamekeeper David Wright who, ironically, had stolen from Hudson and threatened to inform her about Hall's criminal past if Hall dared to tell her. Wright was shot in the back on a game-hunting trip with Hall. Other murder victims included his second high-society employers, Dorothy and Walter Scott-Elliot, who overheard Hall discussing robbing them with an accomplice. Hall then killed their maid, who had helped him dispose of the bodies, after she brazenly wore her dead employer's furs and jewels in public.

CAPTURE

Hall was caught with his half-brother's body, a paedophile he'd murdered purely out of hatred for the man, in the boot of his car.

SENTENCING

He was given a life sentence in 1978 with the recommendation that he should never be released. He died in prison from a stroke.

**1924–2002
LOCATION: UK
DATES ACTIVE: 1977–78
ALSO KNOWN AS:
"THE KILLER BUTLER"
MURDERS: 5**

HARVEY GLATMAN

In Los Angeles in the late 1950s, Glatman was responsible for the abduction, rape and murder of three young women, with a suspected fourth who was linked to him 50 years after his execution.

MEANS

Glatman used a camera to photograph his victims and to help complete his ruse that he was a fashion photographer. He used a gun to threaten them and bound their bodies with rope. After the women were securely tied up, he would strangle them.

MOTIVE

Glatman was inclined towards sadomasochism even before his teenage years. When he was just 12 years old, his parents discovered red welts around his neck from autoerotic asphyxiation. This sexual fascination with strangling apparently extended to other people, too.

OPPORTUNITY

In 1957, he began to lurk outside modelling agencies. He contacted his first victim, 19-year-old Judith Dull, offering her $50 for a pulp-fiction novel cover shoot. Twenty-four-year-old Ruth Mercado was approached in a similar way, except that when the time came for her "photo shoot", she said she was sick and called it off. Glatman drove to her house anyway, forced his way in and raped her at gunpoint, before driving her into the desert and strangling her. Shirley Ann Bridgeford was a 24-year-old divorcée whom Glatman contacted via a lonely hearts newspaper advert. She accepted his offer to take her to a dance, and she was never seen alive again.

CAPTURE

In 1958, a patrolman spotted Glatman in the act of attempting to abduct a woman who, no doubt, would have been his fourth victim, and he was arrested.

SENTENCING

After his arrest, Glatman immediately confessed to the murders. He was found guilty of first-degree murder, sentenced to death and executed in the gas chamber.

**1927–1959
LOCATION: USA
YEARS ACTIVE:
1957–1958
MURDERS: 3+**

DOROTHEA
PUENTE

This murderous landlady took advantage of the fact that not even police detectives suspected her of murder, because of her age and petite stature.

MEANS

As the landlady of a boarding house in Sacramento, California, Dorothea Puente offered lodgings to the elderly and vulnerable – as well as those with addiction problems and perceived as "tough cases" – who were often referred to her by social workers. At any one time, in the boarding house she managed in Sacramento, California, there were more than a dozen people under Puente's care. Soft-spoken and non-threatening, the middle-aged Puente could have been the mother of the men that investigated the frequent disappearances of her tenants and the mysterious smell emanating from her house on F Street.

MOTIVE

Puente was driven by greed: she poisoned her elderly and disabled tenants to con them out of their social security cheques. At its peak, this deplorable source of income was bringing Puente more than $5,000 a month.

OPPORTUNITY

She would collect the mail before her tenants would see it, siphon off any cheques and then pay them a considerably smaller sum. Puente would tell people that she hobnobbed with the celebrities of the time and even that she was related by marriage to champion heavyweight boxer Ingemar Johansson. As Puente was a practised liar, convincing sick or intellectually disabled tenants to drink beverages laced with fatal doses of painkillers was the easy part of her crimes.

CAPTURE

The difficult part was disposing of the mounting number of dead tenants. When police visited to inquire about missing tenant Alberto Montoya, they discovered soil that had recently been disturbed on the plot outside Puente's guesthouse. Fertilizing her avocado tree and flower beds were the corpses of seven of her former tenants.

SENTENCING

A robust defence that described Puente's "caring and generous" side failed to con the jury into a not-guilty verdict. She was convicted of three murders and given a life sentence in 1993. She died in prison from natural causes in 2011.

**1929–2011
LOCATION: USA
ALSO KNOWN AS:
"DEATH HOUSE
LANDLADY"
YEARS ACTIVE:
1982–88
MURDERS: 9+**

ENSIO KOIVUNEN

Koivunen murdered young hitchhikers in the Helsinki area of Finland and had an unusual means of killing his victims.

MEANS

He picked up three young female hitchhikers over the course of a single summer in 1971: Salme Helena Metsänikula, Pirjo Marjatta Laiho and Ritva Anneli Raijas. He drove a Dodge Dart and used it to finish his victims off by poisoning them with exhaust after attacking them. He left one of his victims wrapped up in a plastic sheet in Ingå forest, her shoes tied up and neatly arranged by her body.

MOTIVE

He had a long history of criminality, including burglary, and had also done some jail time. He sexually assaulted the women prior to killing them and stole some of their personal items, including a belt. These were more likely to be keepsakes, taken as souvenirs of his murders, rather than for material gain.

OPPORTUNITY

Each of the murdered women was hitchhiking at the time, and teenagers Pirjo and Ritva were travelling together on their way to Hyvinkää, north of Helsinki. They were witnessed getting into Koivunen's car on a bridge near an Esso petrol station.

CAPTURE

Fingerprint evidence finally linked Koivunen to the women's bodies. He was brought in for questioning, but as a habitual liar, there was no consistency to his story, which changed every time he told it.

SENTENCING

Koivunen was convicted of three counts of negligent homicide, among other charges, and given a 25-year prison sentence.

**1930–2003
LOCATION: FINLAND
YEARS ACTIVE: 1971
MURDERS: 3**

RICHARD KUKLINSKI

Kuklinski was a Mafia hitman who worked for the infamous Five Families of New York City. He likely killed dozens more than the six people he was convicted of murdering and has admitted to killing men ("no women or children") long before he was being paid to do it.

MEANS

Kuklinski was a large man and intimidating figure who could wield his bulk to overpower his victims (most of them criminal associates or enemies of a mobster) and strangle them. He also used a gun, a knife and cyanide poison. As a career killer, he experimented with various methods of murder, honing his technique. He would freeze the bodies of his victims to make it difficult for investigators to ascertain the time of death, which earned him the nickname "The Iceman".

MOTIVE

While Kuklinski scored just below the cutoff on the clinical checklist for gauging psychopathy in individuals, he displayed many of the traits of a psychopath, including complete detachment from the violent murders he committed. He had discovered he was good at killing at 13 years old, when he ambushed and beat to death the leader of a rival gang, Charley Lane. After that, he realized he could make good money from this talent as a Mafia assassin.

OPPORTUNITY

A break in his "career" came in the early 1960s, when Gambino family member Roy DeMeo recruited him for his fledgling crew of Mafia hitmen. Kuklinski was allegedly "tested" when DeMeo ordered him to shoot a member of the public chosen completely at random; Kuklinski didn't hesitate to put a bullet in the back of the unsuspecting stranger's head.

CAPTURE

Kuklinski was known to the New York Police Department and was the prime suspect in many murders by the time he was arrested in 1986. ATF Special Agent Dominick Polifrone went undercover to recruit Kuklinski for the supposed assassination of an associate. After he accepted the contract, the cops moved in.

SENTENCING

He was given five consecutive life terms for each of the murders of which he was convicted, and died in prison.

**1935–2006
LOCATION: USA
ALSO KNOWN AS:
"THE ICEMAN"
YEARS ACTIVE: 1949–1986
MURDERS: 6+**

MARIE FIKÁČKOVÁ

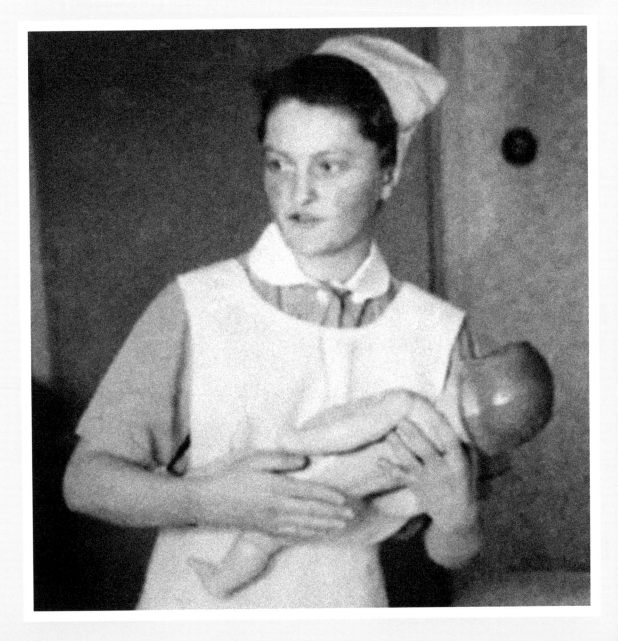

Neonatal nurse Marie Fikáčková admitted to hurting more newborn children than the two for whose deaths she was convicted of murder. It's suspected that she might have killed up to 10 babies.

MEANS

Fikáčková used her bare hands to inflict horrible injuries on at least two newborns at Sušice Hospital, breaking their skulls and limbs to kill them.

MOTIVE

The official reason for the murders was never established, although after six hours of interrogation, Fikáčková said that she felt uncontrollable rage towards the newborn children in her care whenever she was menstruating. She would beat them savagely if they cried, saying that she would "calm down" after attacking them. She came from an extremely poor family and had a difficult relationship with her mother, while her father was a violent alcoholic. Her background likely contributed to the bouts of depression she experienced and her volatile temper.

OPPORTUNITY

Fikáčková had no record prior to the murders, and young children were entrusted to her care. The hospital let the victims down as much as Fikáčková did in her professional capacity as a nurse. There simply weren't enough checks in place – or adequate supervision – to prevent further murders.

CAPTURE

It was only after two babies died in her care on the same day that Fikáčková was arrested, on 27 February 1960.

SENTENCING

She was sentenced to death and executed by hanging on 13 April 1961.

**1936–1961
LOCATION:
CZECHOSLOVAKIA
YEARS ACTIVE:
1957–1960
MURDERS: 2+**

RICHARD MCGOWN

This former doctor was born in Scotland and moved to Zimbabwe in the late 1960s after he graduated. He was convicted of murdering two children but suspected in at least three other suspicious deaths.

MEANS

He injected his two victims with large amounts of morphine, fatal doses for their young bodies.

MOTIVE

McGown had decided to experiment with new methods of pain relief. Perhaps in a country less regulated than Britain and more trusting of his expertise, he felt he could bypass the usual trial procedures and approvals, and experiment on some of his young patients. He handed one of his victims, two-year-old Kalpesh Nagindas, over to his parents saying that he'd "brought him back from the dead", which suggests he might have had a god complex.

OPPORTUNITY

Nagindas and 10-year-old Lavender Khaminwa were brought into his Harare clinic for a circumcision and an appendectomy, respectively. He injected them following the procedures with twice the recommended dose for pain relief, despite the concerns of his nurses. He is thought to have experimented on 500 children in this way.

CAPTURE

After concerns were finally raised in a 1993 report of the deaths of these two children and those of three others, he was arrested.

SENTENCING

McGown was found guilty of two counts of murder but got just a year of prison time, a six-month suspended sentence and a small fine. The UK General Medical Council struck him from the register.

**B.1937
LOCATION: ZIMBABWE
YEARS ACTIVE:
1986–1992
MURDERS: 2+**

IAN BRADY

As one half of Britain's notorious "Moors Murderers", Brady tortured and killed five children with the help of his partner, Myra Hindley. They buried at least two of their victims on Saddleworth Moor, near Manchester.

MEANS

A vehicle featured in all five of Brady's murders, to transport their victim unwittingly to where they would be murdered. Just the presence of Myra Hindley herself facilitated the murders, as the victims would have been less suspicious of a woman or couple than a man alone. Brady used a variety of instruments to murder his victims, including an axe, a serrated knife and a piece of string. He recorded the torture and death of 10-year-old Lesley Ann Downey on audiotape.

MOTIVE

Brady was a psychopath and a sexual sadist, while Hindley was infatuated with her lover and willing to do anything for him, though she would later claim that she was afraid of what Brady might do to her if she didn't help him. The murders were the horrible conclusion of Brady's desire to commit "the perfect murder".

OPPORTUNITY

Brady's victims – Pauline Reade, John Kilbride, Keith Bennett, Lesley Ann Downey and Edward Evans – were each picked up as they walked alone. On each occasion, Brady was driving around with Hindley, specifically hunting for a victim.

CAPTURE

After Hindley's brother-in-law David Smith witnessed the murder of Edward Evans and was asked to help dispose of the body, he called the police. Brady was arrested on 7 October 1965.

SENTENCING

Brady was convicted of three murders (though he confessed to five) and given a life sentence.

**1938–2017
LOCATION: UK
YEARS ACTIVE:
1963–1965
MURDERS: 5**

DEAN ARNOLD CORLL

Corll was a Texan sweet-factory owner with a horrifying taste for teenage boys, torture and murder.

MEANS

Corll's moniker and modus operandi sound like a sick joke: his family owned a sweet factory, of which he was vice president, near Houston, Texas, and in the early 1970s he often hung around outside schools, handing out free sweets to children. He had a recreation room with a pool table installed in the factory. It was here that he was able to recruit both David Brooks and Elmer Wayne Henley to help him lure young teenage boys back to his house on Schuler Street.

MOTIVE

Extreme sexual sadism featured heavily in most of the murders. Corll owned a homemade torture board – a simple sheet of wood with holes drilled in it and handcuffs on ropes threaded though the holes. Struggling with his own sexual identity in a homophobic society, Corll could have been seeking to purge his homosexual urges with violence – to kill a part of himself that he loathed.

OPPORTUNITY

Lulled into a false sense of security by Brooks and Henley – boys their own age – Corll's victims stood no chance. Once they had been convinced to come back to Corll's house, they were pounced upon on arrival and easily subdued.

DEATH

Corll was ultimately shot dead by one of his own protégés, Elmer Wayne Henley, before he could be brought to justice. He had tied Henley up for bringing a girl back to the house. Once Henley had convinced Corll to free him on the promise that he would participate in her murder, he grabbed Corll's .22-calibre pistol and shot him six times.

**1939–1973
LOCATION: USA
ALSO KNOWN AS:
"THE CANDY MAN"
YEARS ACTIVE: 1970–73
MURDERS: 28+**

JERRY BRUDOS

Oregon serial killer Jerry Brudos is known for his shoe and foot fetish that spiralled out of control into murder and necrophilia.

MEANS

At both of his Oregon properties, Brudos owned a garage, an insalubrious man cave that was off limits to his wife and children. As a workshop, it had everything he needed to dismember and store the body parts that fuelled his fantasies. In his garage in the city of Salem, he even had a darkroom where he could develop a private gallery of photos of his victims.

MOTIVE

From an early age, Brudos exhibited a foot fetish. The fascination was unwittingly encouraged by his mother, who scolded her son when she caught him wearing her high heels. This created an alluring taboo that grew and festered as the years passed. He kept appendages from some of his victims, typically a foot or breasts, in a freezer. Possessing a woman in a literal, material sense was important to Brudos. His crimes escalated in severity with each one committed: he began by breaking into houses and stealing women's underwear, then moved to committing sexual assault, and later kidnapping, rape, murder and later dismemberment. Brudos's final murder involved the rape, torture, and murder of Linda Salee, after which he experimented with her body, running an electric current through it.

OPPORTUNITY

Brudos had been on the path to darker crimes for some time when, in January 1968, 19-year-old encyclopaedia salesperson Linda Slawson called at his house. Brudos told her he was interested in buying the entire set and persuaded her to talk it over in his garage, where he strangled her. Then he photographed her, cut off her left foot and dumped her body in the Willamette River. He soon learned the kinds of deception that were effective for luring victims into compromising themselves: he posed as a helpful motorist offering aid, a photographer looking for models and a security guard.

CAPTURE

When his final two victims turned up in the river, a local university student informed the police of a man she had gone on a date with recently, who had talked endlessly about the missing women – Brudos. A visit to Brudos's home did not allay the investigators' suspicions: inside they found wire identical to that used used to tie the victims' bodies to the car parts that would weigh their bodies down in the water, plus incriminating photos, clothes and lists of names and addresses. Police had all the forensic evidence they needed to charge him.

SENTENCING

Brudos received three consecutive life sentences for three counts of first-degree murder.

**1939–2006
LOCATION: USA
YEARS ACTIVE:
1968–69
ALSO KNOWN AS:
"THE LUST KILLER", "THE
SHOE FETISH SLAYER"
MURDERS: 4+**

LAWRENCE
BITTAKER

Bittaker and his accomplice Roy Norris were responsible for a small number of heinous torture-murders of teenage girls over a short period of time in southern California. The instruments they used earned them their moniker.

MEANS

He used a windowless GMC cargo van that he bought specifically to facilitate the transport and murder of hitchhiking girls. Bittaker and Norris installed a bed in the back and even named the van "Murder Mac". Underneath the bed was a toolbox, in which he kept instruments of torture that included hammers and ice picks. He also made some audio recordings of his torture sessions and took some photographs with a Polaroid camera.

MOTIVE

Renowned FBI criminal profiler John Douglas, who wrote the 1995 book *Mindhunter* (on which the hit Netflix show is based), described Bittaker as the most disturbing individual he had ever profiled. He was a calculating and extremely violent sexual sadist, who disclosed his dark fantasies to Norris after the men met in prison. He began to plan the rape and murder of hitchhikers in detail on his release, with Norris's help.

OPPORTUNITY

His first victim, 16-year-old Cindy Schaefer, was dragged into the van near Redondo Beach. His next three victims, Andrea Hall, Jackie Gilliam and Leah Lamp, were hitchhikers who accepted a lift from the men in the van. Shirley Lynette Ledford was abducted in a similar way to Schaefer. Shirley Sanders was kidnapped and raped, but she managed to escape and describe her captors to the police.

CAPTURE

Norris boasted of his part in the murders to a prison friend, who informed the police when he discovered he hadn't made it up. On 20 November 1979, Bittaker was arrested.

SENTENCING

Norris received a term of 45 years to life in exchange for his testimony against Bittaker. Bittaker remains on death row today, though a moratorium on the death penalty declared by Governor Newsom in March 2019 means that no prisoner will be executed while it stands.

**B.1940
LOCATION: USA
ALSO KNOWN AS:
"THE TOOLBOX
KILLER"
YEARS ACTIVE: 1979
MURDERS: 5+**

JOHN WAYNE GACY

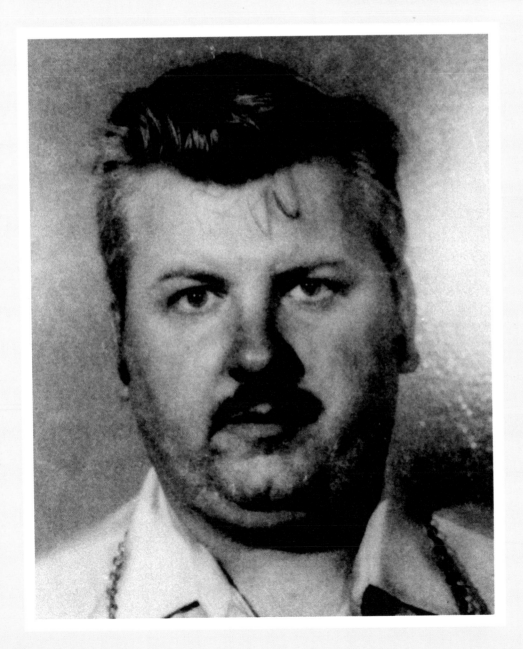

John Wayne Gacy is one of the worst serial killers to come from Chicago, if not the US.

MEANS

Well liked and active in his community of Chicago, Illinois, Gacy was chairman of the Chi Rho Club and on the board of the Catholic Inter-Club Council, as well as several other civic-minded-sounding clubs and societies. One of these was the "Jolly Joker" clown club, which he joined in 1975. It was a charitable organization that entertained sick children, and it gave Gacy a mask that he could slip on when compelled to kill. He had access to chloroform, handcuffs, whips and a homemade pillory.

MOTIVE

It's likely he was seeking the approval of his dead father in his efforts to become a popular and moderately powerful pillar of his community. But his motivation to make contact with as many boys and young men as possible probably spurred him into participating in community affairs more than he would have otherwise. He derived pure pleasure from raping, torturing and murdering his victims. Gacy's torture ritual included whipping the victim and dripping hot candle wax on them, before a rope with a stick thrust through the knot was tied around their neck and twisted slowly until the boy was asphyxiated.

OPPORTUNITY

Gacy had his own construction business, PDM Contractors, and a large part of its workforce comprised teenage boys. As an employer, Gacy had the trust of, and a degree of control over, his employees. He would visit them in their homes when their parents were away, on the pretence that they were being interviewed for a job, or he would choose a time when his wife and stepchildren were away and then call them over to his own home at night. Typically, he plied the boys with alcohol then asked them to put his handcuffs on for a "magic trick". When the boy had locked the handcuffs onto his own wrists, Gacy would tell him, "There's no key ... that's the trick," before chloroforming him unconscious.

CAPTURE

In December 1978, Gacy was already facing a trial for the rape and torture of 26-year-old Jeffrey Rignall, who miraculously survived his ordeal after being left for dead in Chicago's Lincoln Park, when detectives began to link this incident with the murder of pharmacy worker Robert Piest. Gacy was placed under constant surveillance and on 21 December, a second, more thorough search of Gacy's home was conducted. This time investigators made a beeline for the crawl space under the house – from which a Des Plaines police officer detected the telltale stench of rotting flesh. Twenty-six bodies were discovered in the space.

SENTENCING

It took the jury two hours to find Gacy guilty of 33 murders, and he was sentenced to death by lethal injection. The execution date was set to 2 June 1980, but due to several appeals of the case, he spent 14 years on death row before his actual execution on 9 May 1994.

**1942–1994
LOCATION: USA
ALSO KNOWN AS:
"THE KILLER CLOWN"
YEARS ACTIVE: 1972–78
MURDERS: 33+**

Police outside Gacy's home in Cook County, Illinois, December 1978. Twenty-nine bodies were recovered from his home, all but three from the crawl space beneath the house. The house was demolished in April 1979.

MICHEL FOURNIRET

Considered the French equivalent of the infamous British murderer Fred West, Fourniret would abduct, rape and murder teenage girls and a few women, assisted by his wife.

MEANS

Fourniret would drive his victims to a secluded location under the pretence of giving them a lift, the presence of his wife reassuring them. He forced at least one of his victims to swallow Rohypnol – a powerful sedative – and manually strangled them, asphyxiated them with a rope, or shot them with a pistol.

MOTIVE

Most of his murders were sexually motivated but at least one murder, that of Farida Hammiche, was to steal a large sum of gold coins and ingots.

OPPORTUNITY

In 1988, Fourniret helped Farida Hammiche, the wife of a bank robber named Jean-Pierre Hellegouarch, uncover a 20-kilogram stash of gold hidden by her husband before he was jailed. She paid him a handsome cut, but less than a month later he strangled Hammiche, buried her body and then broke into her house in the Parisian suburbs to steal the rest of the gold.

CAPTURE

After Hellegouarch was released in 1992 and discovered Fourniret had bought a stunning eighteenth-century French chateau, he became suspicious. He turned to the police. It still took over a decade and his attempted abduction of a young girl for Fourniret to be arrested in 2003.

SENTENCING

Fourniret was sentenced to life imprisonment without the possibility of parole, in 2008.

**B.1942
LOCATION: FRANCE
ALSO KNOWN AS:
"THE OGRE OF
THE ARDENNES"
YEARS ACTIVE:
1987–2001
MURDERS: 8+**

RODNEY ALCALA

CALIF   PRISON
C 18300
R ALCALA
SQ COND   9 2 97

Alcala was a prolific serial killer who was convicted of murdering seven women and has been charged with the murder of one more, in the states of California, New York and Washington, although he likely killed many more. He got his moniker after it was discovered he had appeared on the television show *The Dating Game* between murders.

MEANS

He often used his bare hands to beat and strangle his victims, choking them unconscious and waiting for them to come around before strangling them again. However, he was known to use blunt weapons also. In 1968, he beat his first known victim, eight-year-old Tali Shapiro, with a steel bar (miraculously, she survived). Alcala would carry a camera to help create the illusion that he was scouting for models.

MOTIVE

Alcala was described by both a military psychiatrist during his time in the Army in the early 1960s, and later by psychiatrists at his trials, as having various personality disorders. He was a narcissist and sexual sadist who took pleasure in the trauma he was able to inflict upon his victims, prolonging it until they died.

OPPORTUNITY

As he honed his methods, he began to pose as a fashion photographer, luring some of his victims away for a private photo shoot. Twelve-year-old Robin Samsoe, from Huntington Beach, California, was last seen alive on the beach with her friends on 20 June 1979, where they were approached by a man who offered to take their photos.

CAPTURE

Alcala was identified and arrested on suspicion of murdering Robin Samsoe after a sketch of the mysterious photographer was circulated.

SENTENCING

After Alcala was sentenced to death twice and had his sentence overturned twice on technicalities, DNA evidence linked him, in 2003, to the murders of four women. This time his conviction stuck, and he was sentenced to death for the murders of Robin Samsoe, Georgia Wixted, Jill Barcomb, Charlotte Lamb, and Jill Parenteau, in March 2010.

**B.1943
LOCATION: USA
ALSO KNOWN AS:
"THE DATING
GAME KILLER"
YEARS ACTIVE:
1968–1979
MURDERS: 8+**

PAUL MICHAEL STEPHANI

Paul Stephani achieved notoriety not so much for the murders he committed, but for the hysterical phone confessions to the emergency services he made immediately after them.

MEANS

Stephani was an approachable, average-looking young guy who did not initially arouse the suspicions of the women he targeted, which included at least one sex worker. The killer used slim, piercing instruments to kill his victims – common tools that could be found in almost any American household, such as an ice pick or a screwdriver.

MOTIVE

After almost all of the attacks, the "Weepy-voiced Killer" would phone the police with a confession in which he would become so distraught his sentences were barely comprehensible. Stephani was raised in a religious family and he might have been seeking absolution for more than just the murders.

OPPORTUNITY

One of his victims, Barbara Simons, trusted him enough to accept his offer of a lift home, remarking to a waitress at the bar they'd met in that he seemed like a nice guy. She was found stabbed to death the next day. Survivor Denise Williams was a sex worker who got into Stephani's car one August evening in 1982. He attacked her with a screwdriver, but she was able to hit him in the face with a glass bottle and flee.

CAPTURE

A witness to the attack on Williams was able to describe the attacker. Meanwhile, Stephani made the mistake of calling for an ambulance for his head wound when he returned home. Through this phone call and the witness description, police were able to link him to the murders.

SENTENCING

Stephani got a 40-year prison term in 1982, and died 16 years later of skin cancer.

**1944–1998
LOCATION: USA
ALSO KNOWN AS:
"THE WEEPY-VOICED
KILLER"
YEARS ACTIVE: 1982–83
MURDERS: 3**

JOHN COOPER

Welshman Cooper was a dangerously unstable and violent killer whose crimes went unpunished for two decades before he was caught.

MEANS

Cooper owned a sawn-off shotgun, which was used in the double murders of siblings Richard and Helen Thomas and married couple Peter and Gwenda Dixon. He knew the area around his Pembrokeshire home well, including the remote coastal paths and settlements where his crimes might not be noticed immediately.

MOTIVE

As a serial robber, burglar and a convicted rapist, violence and criminality were second nature to Cooper. He was a diagnosed psychopath, for whom taking the lives of the people he robbed to cover his tracks required no more thought than flicking a light switch. The manner in which he killed the Dixons is a testament to his complete lack of conscience: they were bound, robbed of £300 cash, and then each executed with a shotgun blast to the face.

OPPORTUNITY

Cooper appeared on a popular TV game show, *Bullseye*, three weeks before he murdered the Dixons in 1989, telling the host how much he enjoyed scuba diving in the coastal waters around his home. He was certainly the outdoorsy type: in his 2011 trial, his son testified to the fact that Cooper would go for long walks armed with a shotgun, including on the days of the murders.

CAPTURE

The case went cold for 20 years, and although Cooper was in prison from 1998 to 2009 on robbery and burglary charges, this gave police time to gather evidence against him for the murders. Ultimately, evidence of the Dixons' blood on Cooper's shotgun linked him to the crimes.

SENTENCING

He was given four life sentences with no chance of parole.

**B. 1944
LOCATION: UK
ALSO KNOWN AS:
"THE BULLSEYE KILLER"
DATES ACTIVE: 1985–89
MURDERS: 4**

IVAN MILAT

Milat gained considerably infamy after seven bodies were found in and around the Belanglo State Forest in New South Wales. The victims were all backpackers, five of them European tourists, and his crimes ended an era of innocence in the Australian backpacker community.

MEANS

He possessed at least one large hunting knife and he also owned a pistol with which he would intimidate his victims for long enough until he could tie them up. He beat some of them with his bare fists. Finally, Milat had a four-wheel drive vehicle to gain access to remote areas with difficult terrain, where his captives would be stabbed or shot, sometimes both. He piled rocks and branches on some of the bodies.

MOTIVE

Investigators found evidence of sexual assault on some of his female victims, but this wasn't Milat's primary motive. He enjoyed the thrill of power that killing gave him. His brother Boris Milat told Australian current affairs program *Sunday Night*, "He was going to kill somebody from the age of 10. It was built into him. He had a different psyche. He's a psychopath, and it just manifested itself with, 'I can do anything, I can do anything'."

OPPORTUNITY

He would cruise up and down part of the Hume Highway looking for hitchhikers and then offer them a lift. Once he'd found a quieter stretch of road, he'd pull in and threaten them with his pistol, telling them that they were being robbed. In 1990, British backpacker Mark Onions managed to escape from a man who fit Milat's description, and who tried to abduct him in exactly this way.

CAPTURE

New South Wales police managed to narrow a list of suspects, using a criminal profile they had developed and a data-linking system that included criminal records and gun licences. Milat was arrested in May 1994, after Mark Onions flew to Australia and positively identified him.

SENTENCING

He was found guilty of all seven murders in 1996, and given life imprisonment without parole for each.

**B.1944
LOCATION:
AUSTRALIA
ALSO KNOWN AS:
"THE BACKPACKER
MURDERER"
YEARS ACTIVE:
1989–1993
MURDERS: 7+**

CHARLES SOBHRAJ

Vietnam-born French national Charles Sobhraj was, at one point in the 1970s, Asia's most notorious serial killer, murdering western backpackers following the popular "Hippie Trail" across Southeast Asia. He is suspected of at least 12 murders.

MEANS

Sobhraj was smart, charming and well dressed – an experienced con artist with a colourful criminal past that included car theft and drug smuggling, before he turned to murder. He amassed a small following of female admirers, some of whom were so besotted with him that they would assist in his crimes. He preferred to drug his victims into a stupor and from there, they were either beaten to death with a wooden plank, had their throats cut, or in one horrific case, that of Vitali Hakim, burned alive.

MOTIVE

Robbery was Sobhraj's primary motive. Drugging and killing these travellers who were so far from home was a safer option than leaving them to sober up and report the crime. He is thought by many to be a psychopath, devoid of empathy.

OPPORTUNITY

Sobhraj would befriend tourists and hippies in Thailand and host parties at his Bangkok mansion, where at least 12 murders took place. He was helped by at least two accomplices: a Canadian girl named Marie-Andrée Leclerc, who had an unrequited crush on him, and an Indian boy named Ajay Chowdhury.

CAPTURE

He was finally caught after failing to poison an entire group of 60 French students in New Delhi in July 1976. The students who didn't fall unconscious realized what he'd done, and tied up both Sobhraj and his accomplices. Sobhraj managed to escape longer prison sentences up until 2003, when he was arrested in Nepal.

SENTENCING

He was sentenced to life imprisonment in 2004 for two murders in 1975. He was convicted of another murder in 2014 and is now in poor health, having had several heart surgeries.

**B.1944
LOCATION: INDIA,
NEPAL AND THAILAND
ALSO KNOWN AS:
"THE SERPENT"
YEARS ACTIVE:
1975–1976
MURDERS: 12+**

LEONARD

THOMAS LAKE

Lake was the alpha partner in a notorious serial torture-murder duo in Calaveras County, California, along with Charles Ng.

MEANS

He rented a cabin that he shared with Ng in the Californian countryside, where he built what he described in his journals as a "dungeon". He was an amateur pornographer who owned recording equipment and whose own marriage had fallen apart because of the bondage films he enjoyed making. Lake collected guns and had been desensitized to violence and bloodshed during two tours in Vietnam as a US Marine, where he saw active combat.

MOTIVE

Lake's acts of prolonged psychological and physical torture on the women he kept in his "dungeon" prior to killing them represent the extremes of a psychopathic serial killer's motives: he wanted to inflict suffering. Lake focused his rape and torture on women, killing any men and infants immediately. In these acts, he was wholly detached from recognizable humanity. In his own journal, Ng drew a crude cartoon of his accomplice holding a baby up by one leg and beating it, before dropping it into a vat – presumably full of acid, as Lake had enjoyed dissolving mice in chemicals as a child. As a pure psychopath, Lake was devoid of empathy, and therefore had no internal checkpoints to halt his voracious pursuit of escalating sexual sadism.

OPPORTUNITY

The hippie lifestyle that was still prevalent in 1980s California drew some of Lake and Ng's victims, looking for work and hoping to live the good life in the West Coast sunshine, to their Wilseyville ranch. Two young families number among the burned remains found near the ranch, including Lake's neighbours Lonnie Bond and Brenda O'Connor and their son Lonnie Jr, who all disappeared in 1983. O'Connor was next seen on one of Lake's videotapes, bound and being told in excruciating detail what was going to happen to her. Most of Lake and Ng's victims knew one or both of them, including neighbours and their friends or family, work colleagues, and even Lake's own brother.

CAPTURE

Lake was arrested in 1985, but he swallowed cyanide pills sewn into his shirt and died four days later. Ng is on death row at San Quentin.

**1945–1985
LOCATION: USA
YEARS ACTIVE:
1983–85
MURDERS: 11+**

DENNIS RADER

Wichita-based home-security engineer Rader was a predatory stalker who broke into his victims' houses, tied them up, tortured and murdered them.

MEANS

His job installing home security meant he knew his way around alarm systems and was better equipped to access secure homes than the average burglar. He used a pistol in at least one case (that of the Otero family, his first murders) to intimidate his victims, and then rope to bind them. He asphyxiated some of his victims with plastic bags, hung some with rope and manually strangled others.

MOTIVE

Rader's sexual deviance began in his teens, with an interest in sadomasochistic pornography that developed into stealing underwear for his private collection and spying into women's bedrooms. He started to want to hurt people in his late 20s, trying bondage with prostitutes at first until, by his own admission, he became "too scary" for them and they refused to see him again. He seemed to relish the notoriety of his crimes, taunting police and the press with letters and enjoying the publicity that "BTK" was receiving. This was an additional part of the payoff for Rader, after the sexual gratification of his murders.

OPPORTUNITY

Having selected his victim, he would carefully plan the murders, preparing his kit and observing the victim's house to get a sense of their daily routine. For his first four murders, those of the Otero family on the evening of 15 January 1974, he waited until nine-year-old Joseph Otero opened the door, to gain access to the house. For others, he would break into the house and wait until his victim returned home.

CAPTURE

After Rader posted a floppy disk to a TV station, a police digital forensic team recovered data that identified him. Familial DNA recovered from his daughter Kerri's pap smear test corroborated this evidence, and Rader was arrested in February 2005.

SENTENCING

Rader was given consecutive life sentences for each of his murders.

**B.1945
LOCATION: USA
ALSO KNOWN AS: "BTK"
(BIND, TORTURE, KILL)
YEARS ACTIVE:
1974–1991
MURDERS: 10**

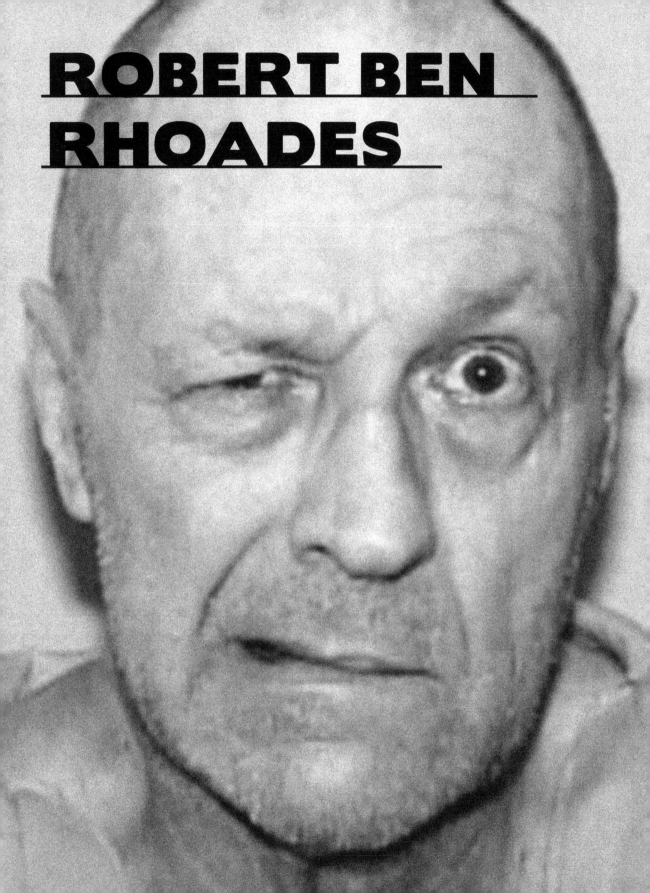

ROBERT BEN RHOADES

Truck driver Rhoades was convicted of three murders but suspected of many more, based on the routes he took for his work and the unsolved murders and people who have gone missing along those routes at the same time.

MEANS

He had converted the sleeper cab in the back of his truck into a makeshift torture chamber, equipped with handcuffs on the ceiling. He kept a rape-and-torture kit that included a whip, a chain, alligator clips, a dildo and a leash. He used baling wire – the sort used to bind hay – to hang Regina Walters and took photos of her prior to her death. He shot Candace Walsh.

MOTIVE

Rhoades was driven by extreme sexual sadism. Candace Walsh and Regina Walters were held in his torture chamber and repeatedly raped and assaulted over the course of a week (and probably longer in Walters's case) before they were murdered. Douglas Zyskowski and Ricky Lee Jones, the male companions to two women, were murdered soon after they had accepted a lift from Rhoades.

OPPORTUNITY

Candace Walsh and Douglas Zyskowski were hitchhiking in Texas in 1990, when Rhoades stopped his truck to pick them up. Regina Walters and Ricky Jones were runaway teens, also hitchhiking in Texas, when they caught a lift with the murderous trucker just a month after Rhoades had murdered Walsh and Zyskowski.

CAPTURE

He was arrested in Arizona after State Trooper Mike Miller encountered his truck parked up on the side of Interstate 10, just outside Casa Grande, in April 1990. Miller spotted a woman in distress inside the truck and arrested Rhoades.

SENTENCING

He was convicted of the murders of Candace Walsh, Douglas Zyskowski and Regina Walters (Ricky Jones's body has never been found) and given life without parole.

**B.1945
LOCATION: USA
ALSO KNOWN AS: "THE
TRUCK STOP KILLER"
YEARS ACTIVE:
1975–1990
MURDERS: 3+**

DENNIS NILSEN

Scottish serial killer Nilsen murdered at least 12 young men at two separate north London addresses. His case gained particular notoriety in the UK after body parts were discovered in the drain outside his Muswell Hill flat.

MEANS

Nilsen would ply his victims with alcohol at his flat and then strangle them with his hands or a ligature, or attempt to drown them in his bath or kitchen sink. He would store their bodies beneath the floorboards or in the bath for a time, before applying his knowledge of butchery, as a former British Army chef, to dismember his victims. Some of those body parts were stashed in plastic bags and stored in his flat, some were flushed down the drain, and others he burned in a fire in his garden.

MOTIVE

Nilsen had harboured fantasies of having sex with an unconscious or dead man for years before he murdered his first known victim, 14-year-old Stephen Dean Holmes. He was later described by a psychiatrist as having a narcissistic personality disorder with "schizoid disturbances" that left him unable to control certain impulses. This was likely exacerbated by the extreme loneliness he felt after he experienced several painful breakups and years of repressing his true sexuality.

OPPORTUNITY

All of Nilsen's victims willingly accompanied him back to his flat, some after he had struck up a conversation with them at one of the pubs he frequented, like The Cricklewood Arms, or The Golden Lion pub in Soho, central London. It was simply a matter of him convincing them to drink heavily, or for Nilsen to wait until they fell asleep, before he attacked them.

CAPTURE

When an emergency plumber investigating a blocked drain outside 23 Cranley Gardens turned up decomposing human flesh, police traced it directly into Nilsen's flat, where they found further human remains.

SENTENCING

Nilsen was convicted of six murders and two attempted murders. He was given a life sentence with a minimum of 25 years.

**1945–2018
LOCATION: UK
ALSO KNOWN AS:
"THE MUSWELL HILL
MURDERER"
YEARS ACTIVE:
1978–1983
MURDERS: 12+**

ROBERT BLACK

One of the UK's most notorious paedophile serial killers hailed from Scotland, but used his job as a cover to hunt for vulnerable young children across the entire UK.

MEANS

Black delivered posters for an East London firm in the 1970s. He was willing to take on gruelling long-distance deliveries across the UK that were much less attractive to his colleagues. He took extra care to obscure his identity with dark glasses, different spectacles and by alternating his style of facial hair. He fitted curtains across the windows of his van to deter prying eyes.

MOTIVE

Four years before his capture, FBI criminal psychologists profiled him as a "desperate ... man whose need for little children is greater than his fear of being exposed as a paedophile". Prosecutor John Milford was more explicit in his opening speech at trial on 13 April 1994: "Each victim was obviously taken for sexual gratification. Susan Maxwell's pants were removed, Caroline Hogg was naked and Sarah Harper was found to have suffered injury."

OPPORTUNITY

We know from the testimony of would-be abductee Teresa Thornhill that Black's method was akin to an ambush. He would choose an opportune moment on a quiet street to drive up to his victim, attempt to gain her trust, then bundle her into his van when her guard was down, and drive away.

CAPTURE

Black was spotted in the middle of a kidnapping. On high alert for child abductions along the Scottish Borders, six police cars stopped Black's van leaving the town. A six-year-old girl, Mandy, was found inside. She had been sexually assaulted and was bound and bruised – but alive.

SENTENCING

Black was convicted of four murders and given a life sentence with a minimum term of 35 years.

**1947–2016
LOCATION: UK
YEARS ACTIVE:
1981–1986
MURDERS: 4+**

THEODORE "TED" ROBERT BUNDY

Probably the most notorious serial killer in history, Ted Bundy had a reputation for lulling his victims into a false sense of security before murdering them.

MEANS

Ted Bundy possessed a perfect storm of traits that allowed him to kill over and over again. He was middle class and white, which in 1970s America made him less suspicious than those born into lower classes and of different ethnicities. He was intelligent and studied psychology and law, which gave him an edge in approaching victims and eluding apprehension. Since his trial, Bundy has been characterized by his charm, which was a skill that helped him to catch his victims off guard, slip through the fingers of law enforcement and hide his crimes from those closest to him.

MOTIVE

His pathology has proved difficult for experts to define, but total domination of his female victims was a part of his compulsion to kill. Bundy was a pure psychopath in the sense that he understood he was inflicting pain and suffering, and saw nothing wrong with it. Bundy felt it was his right to rape, torture and murder young women. And once he had taken his victims to a secluded spot, they infuriated him simply by their willingness to stay alive. "I can kill you whenever I want," he screamed at survivor Rhonda Stapley, "You should be thanking me that you're even breathing air." He was bemused by the witnesses who testified against him, and told psychiatrist Dorothy Lewis, "I don't know why everyone is out to get me."

OPPORTUNITY

Bundy owned a brown Volkswagen Beetle that he would drive around college campuses and student communities. As in the case of Rhonda Stapley, his victims were often naive young hitchhikers. He would also lure women into a false sense of security by pretending his car was broken down, or he had a broken limb and needed help moving a large item into his car. Once his intended victim was occupied with loading the boot up, he would knock them unconscious.

CAPTURE

Bundy was apprehended and convicted of aggravated kidnapping, but escaped. He was caught again, but escaped for a second time. He subsequently attacked five young women (two who died, three who sustained horrific injuries) and murdered 12-year-old Kimberley Leach. After this brutal spree, Bundy was finally caught attempting to flee the area.

SENTENCING

He received three death sentences, but didn't go to the electric chair until nearly a decade after sentencing.

**1946–1989
LOCATION: USA
YEARS ACTIVE: 1974–78
MURDERS: 30+**

Leon County Sheriff Ken Katsaris
reads the indictment charging
Bundy with the murders of two
coeds at the Chi Omega house.
Bundy's attitude throughout this
trial was casual and confident.

KENNETH MCDUFF

As a young man, McDuff was responsible for the abduction and cold-blooded murders of three teenagers in Everman, Texas. His case gained particular infamy when he was considered "rehabilitated" and released after serving less than 20 years in prison; he went on to kill again.

MEANS

McDuff used a pistol to execute 17-year-old Robert Brand and his 15-year-old cousin Mark Dunman, before using a three-foot length of broomstick to choke Brand's 16-year-old girlfriend, Edna Louise Sullivan, to death. He abducted them in their own Ford while his accomplice, Roy Green, followed in McDuff's Dodge Coronet. For the murders he committed following his release, McDuff often used a vehicle to drive his victim away to a place where he could rape and murder them without being disturbed.

MOTIVE

He was a sadist, sexual predator, narcissist and psychopath, for whom the female victims he selected were there to be "used up", according to the testimony of one of his accomplices, Hank Worley. After his second trial in 1992, he was described by renowned Dallas psychologist Fred Labowitz as "a guy with no soul".

OPPORTUNITY

McDuff was cruising around in his Dodge Coronet in 1966 looking for a girl when he spotted Edna Sullivan and her two male companions. Though this was purely a case of being in the wrong place at the wrong time, some of his later victims were sex workers or lone women.

CAPTURE

After being released in 1989 following a parole board's dubious conclusion that he could still contribute to society, McDuff murdered at least six more women across Texas, before a co-worker at a waste-disposal company recognized him from his mugshot on the TV program *America's Most Wanted*. He was arrested in 1992.

SENTENCING

He was sentenced to death for the final time in 1993 and executed by lethal injection five years later.

**1946–1998
LOCATION: USA
ALSO KNOWN AS:
"THE BROOMSTICK
KILLER"
YEARS ACTIVE:
1966–1991
MURDERS: 9+**

HAROLD
SHIPMAN

After the suspicious death of a patient at a GP surgery in Hyde, near Manchester, Dr Shipman became national news headlines in the UK in the late 1990s. Over 200 murders of mostly elderly female patients were linked to Shipman over 20 years of his career. By number of confirmed victims, he is the world's most prolific serial killer.

MEANS

A respected doctor, Shipman had the trust of his patients, who allowed him to inject them with fatal doses of diamorphine. As a general practitioner, he had access to these controlled medicines, the knowledge and experience to administer doses he knew would be fatal, and the authority to sign death certificates noting natural causes of death with relative impunity. He used a typewriter to forge wills.

MOTIVE

Shipman defrauded his victims' families of thousands of pounds (tens of thousands in some cases) of inheritance, forging signatures and turning wills in his favour as the "good doctor". This was considered his primary motive, although criminal psychiatrists – to whom Shipman refused to speak – assume that he had a "god complex", revelling in the power of life and death he had over his patients.

OPPORTUNITY

Shipman's last known victim, Kathleen Grundy, was murdered in a similar fashion to many of his other patients. He made a home visit to the 81-year-old's cottage on 24 June 1998. Once there, he administered a "booster" injection then left, allowing Grundy to slip into a coma and die.

CAPTURE

Grundy's daughter, a solicitor, was shocked both that her mother had died suddenly of "old age" despite being in good health and that her mother's doctor was the beneficiary of Grundy's £386,000 estate. She began to make inquiries and discovered that a suspiciously high number of Shipman's patients had died, leaving him large sums in their wills. After Shipman's fingerprints were found on Grundy's will, her body was exhumed and morphine found in her system. Shipman was arrested on 7 September 1998.

SENTENCING

Shipman was convicted of 15 murders and given a life sentence.

**1946–2004
LOCATION: UK
ALSO KNOWN AS:
"DOCTOR DEATH"
YEARS ACTIVE:
1975–1998
MURDERS: 218+**

EDMUND KOLANOWSKI

Kolanowski

własnoręczny podpis ubezpieczonego

Kolanowski was a necrophile who killed two females (a 21-year-old woman and an 11-year-old girl) in Poznań, western Poland, and a 20-year-old woman in Poland's capital, Warsaw. He took parts of their bodies and sewed them onto mannequins upon which he would perform various sex acts.

MEANS

He wielded a heavy branch to bludgeon his first victim to death, and stabbed two later victims. With a knife, he mutilated their bodies and cut away their genitals and breasts. He used scraps of material, a needle and thread to create dolls onto which these body parts were sewn.

MOTIVE

Kolanowski discovered from an early age that he was sexually aroused by corpses. His father drank himself into an early grave and his brother died at the age of two, after which his mother regularly took her young son to Miłostowo cemetery. Here, he observed the bodies of women in the chapel, which excited him.

OPPORTUNITY

He met his first victim at a lonely railway station in Poznań in 1970. It was over a decade before he encountered his second victim in Warsaw and his final victim was murdered just nine months after that.

CAPTURE

Not long after being seen masturbating over the corpses in the chapel in Miłostowo cemetery in May 1983, Kolanowski was arrested. He was linked to his final victim by a piece of paper he dropped at the crime scene which led police to the factory where he worked.

SENTENCING

His trial concluded in June 1985, and he was sentenced to death and executed by hanging in July 1986.

**1947–1986
LOCATION: POLAND
YEARS ACTIVE:
1970–1982
MURDERS: 3**

EDMUND KEMPER

4 28 73   29026

Kemper murdered and dismembered young female college students in and around various campuses in California. He engaged in various necrophilic acts with most of his victims and ended his horrible crimes by killing his own mother.

MEANS

Kemper was an unusually large man – 6 feet 9 inches tall (205 cm) and reportedly weighing around 145 kilograms – and his victims were as easily manipulated as dolls in his hands. Some he strangled to death, but he still used weapons in some of the murders: a .22-calibre pistol, a knife, and in the case of his mother, a claw hammer. He was also exceptionally bright: his IQ of 145 was as much an asset to him in the commission of his murders as his size.

MOTIVE

Kemper had displayed some of the hallmarks of a serial killer in his childhood, killing small animals and storing the parts in his wardrobe for his mother to find. He decapitated his sister's dolls and he once stalked his teacher with a bayonet. His abusive mother was afraid of her own child, who was well over six feet tall in his early teens, and made him sleep in the locked basement at night. He shot his grandparents dead when he was 15, for which he served five years in a hospital for the criminally insane. When tried for his later crimes, Kemper himself told the court that he wanted to "possess" the women he killed, like objects, and he also blamed his mother for his crimes. He told psychiatrists that he'd realized he'd been trying to kill his mother all along, and decided his final crime would be to kill her before he handed himself in.

OPPORTUNITY

Kemper's Ford Galaxie bore a university staff parking sticker (belonging to his mother, who worked at Santa Cruz), making it relatively easy for him to pick up hitchhiking university students who, with a suspected serial killer in the area, had been told only accept lifts from other students or college employees.

CAPTURE

After murdering his mother and her friend on 20 April 1973, he fled the state – before having a change of heart and handing himself in.

SENTENCING

Kemper was given concurrent life sentences for each of the murders.

**B.1948
LOCATION: USA
ALSO KNOWN AS:
"THE CO-ED KILLER"
YEARS ACTIVE:
1972–1973
MURDERS: 10**

A handcuffed Kemper with a detective outside Pueblo District Court, Colorado. The law finally caught up with Kemper in Pueblo, where he called police from a phone booth to confess.

ROBERT PICKTON

Robert Pickton and his brother were wealthy owners of a pig farm not far from Vancouver, on which Pickton tortured and murdered at least six people.

MEANS

He used handcuffs to restrain his victims, then strangled them with his hands or a wire garrotte. He injected some with windscreen washing fluid, and shot others with either a .22-calibre revolver or a .357 Magnum. His abattoir was well equipped to eviscerate and dismember their bodies, the tools of which Pickton was familiar with as a pig farmer who butchered animals. He disposed of some of the bodies by feeding parts to his pigs.

MOTIVE

Having been brought up with the slaughterhouse on site, Pickton was comfortable with the sights and smells of blood and viscera, as well as the sounds of dying animals. More than that, he found comfort in these familiar experiences. He could only be completely satisfied from a sexual encounter if he killed his partner.

OPPORTUNITY

The poorly maintained site where he lived and ran the farm was known for hosting unlicensed parties, for which Pickton would hire sex workers from nearby Vancouver – women who were witnessed arriving at the farm but not leaving. Because of their profession, Pickton thought these women were less likely to be missed, and he considered them disposable.

CAPTURE

After police executed a search warrant on the farm for illegal weapons in 2002, items belonging to missing women were found, including clothing. He was arrested on 22 February and charged with murder.

SENTENCING

Pickton was given a life sentence without the possibility of parole for 25 years.

**B.1949
LOCATION: CANADA
YEARS ACTIVE:
1995–2002
MURDERS: 6+**

AINO NYKOPP-KOSKI

Nykopp-Koski was a nurse who murdered five elderly patients in her care and attempted to murder five more, at nursing homes and hospitals over the course of five years.

MEANS

She administered fatal doses of sedatives, including opiates, to her victims, who had no prescription for the medication.

MOTIVE

No official motive was ever established and Nykopp-Koski refused to confess to any of her crimes, saying that the patients had taken an overdose of their own volition. Court-appointed psychiatrists established that Nykopp-Koski was a psychopath with an anti-social personality disorder, which could account for other minor offences that included aggravated assault and theft. She was, however, in complete control and understood the gravity of her actions at the time.

OPPORTUNITY

As a nurse, Nykopp-Koski had access to medicines at the hospital. Her victims were bed-ridden and after she had administered the fatal dose, she would wait for the symptoms of poisoning to appear before calling in the emergency. "She tried to use these calls to ensure that no one would suspect her," state prosecutor Leena Metsäpelto told the court.

CAPTURE

A pattern of suspicious overdoses was finally linked to Nykopp-Koski, and she was arrested in 2009.

SENTENCING

Nykopp-Koski pleaded not guilty to all the murders, but she was found guilty and sentenced to life imprisonment in 2010.

**B.1950
LOCATION: FINLAND
YEARS ACTIVE:
2004–2009
MURDERS: 5**

KENNETH
BIANCHI

Bianchi was one half of a Californian serial-killing pair known for the "Hillside Strangler" murders, responsible for a dozen abductions and murders in Los Angeles.

Bianchi happened to be in possession of a fake Los Angeles Police Department badge. Accompanied by his cousin, Angelo Buono, he would flash this badge to young women from Buono's car, under the pretence that they were undercover police officers. Bianchi had applied for an LAPD job and had even been for ride-alongs with the police, so he knew what to say and how to act like a cop. Both were familiar with the area, and knew that the no-man's land between Eagle Rock and Glendale would be a good place to dump bodies.

Bianchi suffered from epilepsy-like seizures when he was young, he frequently wet himself as an older child, had a short fuse, and was diagnosed with a personality disorder at 10 years old. His adoptive father died when he was 13 years old, and he began to look up to his elder cousin, Angelo, who boasted about his sexual exploits and "putting women in their place". This resonated with Bianchi, who sought to control women – first by pimping them, then by moving on to rape and murder. A religious upbringing meant he sought impossibly high standards from women, and a flicker of anything he perceived as infidelity or frailty felt crushingly disappointing for Bianchi. When the "Hillside Strangler" duo murdered Karen Mandic and Diane Wilder, they had been "experimenting" with torture methods that included electrocution and lethal injections – Bianchi's twisted means of venting his frustrations.

OPPORTUNITY

There was a witness to at least one of the abductions. From her window, neighbour Beulah Stofer saw 18-year-old Lauren Wagner get into an altercation with two men before being dragged into their car. Bianchi and Buono likely had an easier time approaching victims, and coaxing them into a car, when they were impersonating police officers.

CAPTURE

The murders were finally traced to the pair in 1979, when they were arrested.

SENTENCING

Bianchi received a life term, but is eligible for parole in 2025. Buono was sentenced to life without parole and died in prison.

**B. 1951/1934–2002
LOCATION: USA
ALSO KNOWN AS:
"THE HILLSIDE
STRANGLERS"
YEARS ACTIVE: 1977–78
MURDERS: 12**

DAVID & CATHERINE BIRNIE

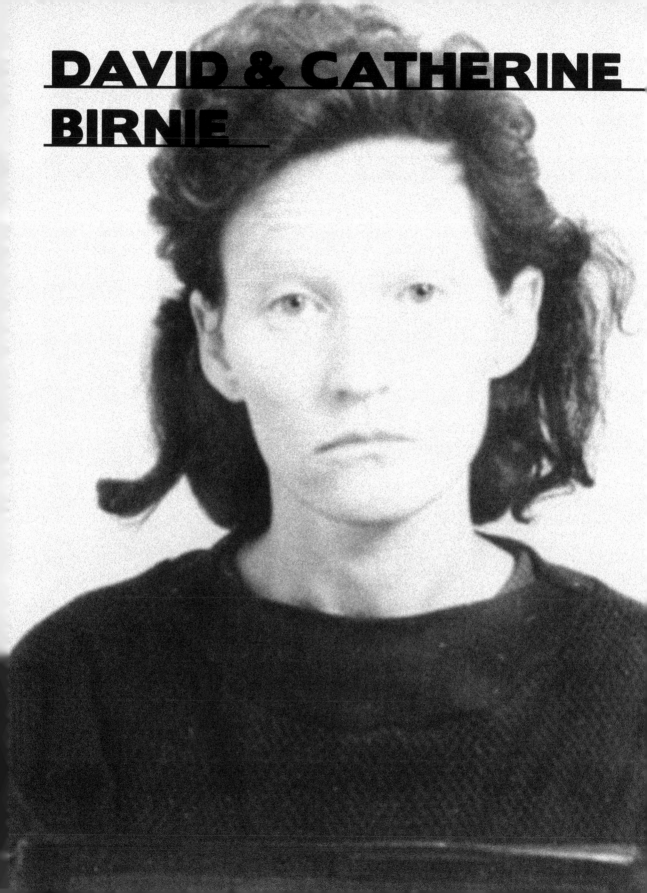

Perth-born Birnie and his wife Catherine would cruise the highways in Western Australia looking for potential victims.

MEANS

They had lived in the Perth area their entire lives and were familiar with places where they could dispose of bodies. For at least a year before they killed their first known victim, Mary Neilson, they had practised kidnapping and murdering, both to become more effective at it and to muster the nerve to go through with it.

MOTIVE

This *folie à deux* couple were sexually motivated: rape and murder was a long-held fantasy of David Birnie, while Catherine Birnie was willing to do anything to please her husband: "I was prepared to follow him to the end of the earth and do anything to see that his desires were satisfied," she later told investigators.

OPPORTUNITY

The Birnies would spend hours actively seeking potential victims. Fifteen-year-old Susannah Candy was hitchhiking on the Stirling Highway when she disappeared, 31-year-old Noelene Patterson's car had broken down, and 21-year-old Denise Brown was waiting for a bus. Seventeen-year-old survivor Kate Moir was also hitchhiking when she was kidnapped, but was later able to escape and inform the police after breaking a window lock in the Birnie home.

CAPTURE

The Birnies were arrested in November 1986, immediately following Kate Moir's escape.

SENTENCING

David Birnie pleaded guilty to all four murder charges levelled at him. The Birnies each received four life sentences. David hanged himself in his cell in 2005.

**1951–2005 / B.1951
LOCATION:
AUSTRALIA
DATES ACTIVE:
OCTOBER –
NOVEMBER 1986
MURDERS: 4+**

JOHANN "JACK" UNTERWEGER

Unterweger was a journalist who killed in his native Austria and the US to create exclusive stories he would then write about.

MEANS

Johann "Jack" Unterweger established his modus operandi in 1974 when he garrotted Margaret Schäfer, his first victim, with her own bra. He was sentenced to life in prison. In the broader sense of having the means to commit his crimes, he was facilitated by liberal writers and artists who, in 1986, successfully petitioned for his release following a stream of literary work Unterweger published while serving time for Schäfer's murder. This included his autobiography, which was based on the conceit that he had become a changed man behind bars. Unterweger's influential supporters argued that he had been rehabilitated, which proved to be far from the truth.

MOTIVE

Unterweger's criminal history was as prolific and varied as his writing. Prior to murder, he was involved in multiple acts of theft and burglary, and had convictions for pimping and sexually assaulting women, so he was no stranger to misogyny. After his 1990 release, he sought the limelight by appearing on television programs to discuss criminal rehabilitation, and even reported news for Austrian television and radio. As it turned out, he had the scoop on a number of murders – because he had committed them himself.

OPPORTUNITY

He targeted sex workers; seven women were murdered in Austria and later, when he was sent to Los Angeles to report on prostitution there, he was shown around the red-light districts. Three more women were strangled with their bras while he was in town.

CAPTURE

The FBI arrested him in Florida in 1992, after Austrian police issued an international warrant for his arrest.

SENTENCING

After being convicted of nine murders and sentenced to life imprisonment without the possibility of parole, Unterweger committed suicide the night of his sentencing.

**1950–1994
LOCATION:
AUSTRIA/USA
DATES ACTIVE: 1974–92
MURDERS: 10+**

BRUCE
MCARTHUR

McArthur was a landscape gardener responsible for a series of murders of men from Toronto's gay community, burying their bodies in various locations across the city.

MEANS

He had user profiles on multiple gay dating platforms, including SilverDaddies, Grindr and BearForest, which he used to arrange meetings with some of his victims. They were beaten and strangled to death. McArthur used a camera to take photos of some of their bodies, posing them in hats and fur coats. Six of his victims were buried in large planters stored with his landscaping tools at a client's house.

MOTIVE

His own repressed homosexuality had a part to play in McArthur's crimes: he was from a strict Christian background that compelled him to keep his sexual orientation at bay until long after his parents died. He left his wife and came out in the 1990s, and in 2001 he seriously assaulted a male sex worker with an iron pipe. He enjoyed being the dominant partner, but was observed to have an explosive temper in the years before his first known murder.

OPPORTUNITY

McArthur's victims were all vulnerable men except one. Six were immigrants or refugees from countries where their sexuality could have landed them in prison or worse. Some were approached in bars or on dating websites, or had been in a relationship with McArthur for some time.

CAPTURE

After a serial killer was suspected in a series of missing men, police linked two of the missing people to McArthur. He was hastily arrested after a young man was seen entering his property in January 2018.

SENTENCING

He was given a life sentence without the possibility of parole for 25 years.

B.1951
LOCATION: CANADA
YEARS ACTIVE: 2010–2017
MURDERS: 8

LENNY MURPHY

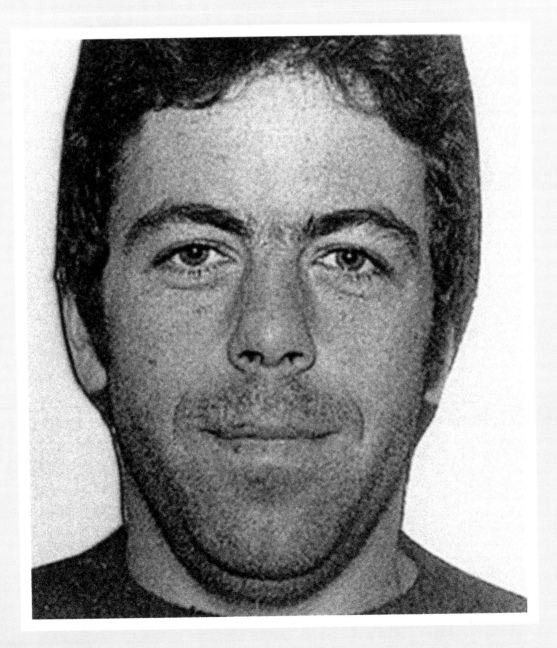

Around the height of the Troubles in 1970s Northern Ireland, Murphy headed up a terrorist gang known as the Shankill Butchers, who characterized themselves by the violent murders of ordinary Catholics in the Shankill area of Belfast.

MEANS

They would use knives and meat cleavers, stolen from the meat-processing plant that gang member William Moore once worked at, and often anything that came to hand to administer a vicious beating to their victims. Then Murphy or one of his lieutenants would use a gun to finish the job.

MOTIVE

In an era when violence and murder was commonplace in Northern Ireland, the extreme prejudice with which Murphy and his gang executed random members of the public shocked Unionists and the IRA alike. Murphy himself had begun his journey into the normalization of escalating violence as a vicious bully at school. Against the backdrop of blood and death in Belfast, committing murder must have seemed like an utterly ordinary thing to do for Murphy.

OPPORTUNITY

Their modus operandi was to use gang member William Moore's taxi to cruise the streets in a Catholic area searching for potential victims, who were identified purely by the sectarian geography. In the case of Francis Cossen, who was simply walking down the street in the early hours of the morning in November 1975, he was coshed with a blunt instrument and dragged off to be beaten and stabbed. Murphy also instigated drive-by shootings and kangaroo court executions. The Shankill Butchers operated more like a hit squad of street criminals than an organized terrorist cell.

CAPTURE

Even the Ulster loyalists – whose cause the Butchers had adopted – regarded Murphy as out of control and a liability. In 1982, Unionists passed details of his movements to the IRA, who executed Murphy in his car on 16 November 1982.

**1952–1982
LOCATION: UK
YEARS ACTIVE:
1972–1982
MURDERS: 23+**

NIKOLAI DZHUMAGALIEV

Dzhumagaliev was a cannibal serial killer whose victims were mostly women, murdered in modern-day Kazakhstan and Russia.

MEANS

He often used a sharp knife to stab his victim or cut their throat, then used the blade to dismember them. An oven was used to cook some body parts, while others were pickled in jars.

MOTIVE

Dzhumagaliev had piquerism – an obsession with penetrating the flesh of his victims – brought on by sexual inadequacy and possible impotence. He found sexual intercourse repulsive; murdering in this way, with the intimacy he achieved by butchering and consuming his victims' bodies, was his means of sexual release. He was also schizophrenic.

OPPORTUNITY

His first known victim was a woman encountered along a path in southeast Kazakhstan. The most brazen murder happened when Dzhumagaliev invited friends over for dinner, killed one of them in a room next to the dining room and was then caught literally red-handed.

CAPTURE

After being arrested and escaping while in transit to a mental institution in 1989, he was caught for the final time in 1991, after being picked up for stealing a sheep in what is now eastern Uzbekistan.

SENTENCING

Dzhumagaliev was declared insane and unfit to stand trial and sent to a fortified treatment centre in southeast Kazakhstan.

**B.1952
LOCATION: USSR
ALSO KNOWN AS:
"METAL FANG"
YEARS ACTIVE: 1979–1991
MURDERS: 10+**

VLADO TANESKI

Taneski became famous after it emerged that he was responsible for the murders in his hometown of Kičevo that he had written about as a crime reporter for the local newspaper.

MEANS

Each of Taneski's three known victims had been bound with a telephone cord. He then beat them and strangled them with the cord. He wrapped the bodies in plastic bags and dumped them at landfill sites or woodlands around the town.

MOTIVE

Taken at face value, it looked as if Taneski was simply creating his own exclusive crime stories, featuring details that no other reporter had access to. With the hindsight of his background, a deeper, Freudian revenge becomes a possible motive: Taneski had been laid off from the newspaper that employed him in 2002, while his wife of 31 years had been promoted and had moved to the capital, Skopje, in the north. Moreover, Taneski's disciplinarian mother had accidentally overdosed in 2002, and all three of his known victims – Mitra Simjanoska, Ljubica Licoska and Zivana Temelkoska – were older women who worked as cleaners, just like his mother.

OPPORTUNITY

Mitra Simjanoska and Ljubica Licoska were walking alone to town when they were abducted. Zivana Temelkoska was lured away from her house by a hoax telephone call from the hospital.

CAPTURE

The details in the stories Taneski sold to the local newspapers were vivid. Police were immediately suspicious of this reporter who "knew too much" after he wrote about the exact type of cord used to bind the women, and that it was also used to strangle them. He was arrested in June 2008.

SENTENCING

Taneski committed suicide in his jail cell the day after he had been arrested.

**1952–2008
LOCATION: NORTH
MACEDONIA
YEARS ACTIVE: 2005–2008
MURDERS: 3+**

OLEKSANDR BERLIZOV

Berlizov was a serial rapist and murderer who terrorized his home city of Dnipropetrovsk, in the central part of the Ukrainian SSR.

MEANS

He strangled his victims to death with his bare hands, a rope or (in one case) the scarf the victim was wearing. He used the cover of darkness to obscure his face.

MOTIVE

Sexual dominance and control over his victims was Berlizov's primary motivation; he was recognized as a sexual psychopath at his trial. He would choke them unconscious before raping them, only strangling them to death if they regained consciousness and he feared them identifying him.

OPPORTUNITY

Berlizov often attacked from behind, at night and in quiet places where he was much less likely to be disturbed. He was also secretary of a local Young Communist League (a respected and secretive Soviet organization) and had volunteered to help hunt for the "maniac", giving him insider knowledge of police searches that allowed him to evade capture. One victim, "Elena", was attacked in her home while on maternity leave. She came to while Berlizov was raping her but feigned unconsciousness, survived the attack and was able to give a description to the police.

CAPTURE

Anatoly Tokar, deputy head of Dnipropetrovsk's Internal Affairs office, led "Elena" around the city hoping she would spot her attacker – and they got lucky. Berlizov escaped, but the authorities were able to link the face to his factory workplace and get a name. Berlizov's apartment was searched, turning up more evidence in the form of trophies – lipsticks, a mirror, a brush – taken from his victims. He was arrested in 1972.

SENTENCING

Berlizov was quickly found guilty of nine murders, sentenced to death by firing squad and executed the same year of his arrest.

**UNKNOWN–1972
LOCATION:
UKRAINIAN SSR
ALSO KNOWN AS:
"THE NIGHT DEMON"
YEARS ACTIVE: 1969–1972
MURDERS: 9**

ROBIN GECHT

As a member of the "Ripper Crew", Gecht would identify and target young women to rape and murder in Chicago, Illinois.

MEANS

Robin Gecht and three other members of a murderous cult would cruise Chicago, Illinois, and its suburbs in a red utility van. Inside, they kept a crude murder kit that included a wire garrotte, handcuffs, knives and a box in which grim "trophies" were stored.

MOTIVE

As a supposed Satanic cult, there was a ritualistic element to each murder. Gecht called his home a "chapel", where the victims were raped before one or of both their breasts were amputated and partly eaten. It's interesting and disturbing to note that Gecht once worked for serial killer John Wayne Gacy's construction company, and the murders began a year after Gacy was arrested.

OPPORTUNITY

Sex workers were commonly targeted as victims by Gecht and his crew because of the ease with which they could be lured to the van. But the Ripper Crew were opportunistic killers, and women who happened to be in the wrong place at the wrong time, like realtor Lorraine Borowski, also became their prey.

CAPTURE

The vile quartet finally slipped up when one of their victims, Beverley Washington, survived despite being horribly mutilated. She was able to give a description of her would-be killers, which led the police to a former address of the Ripper Crew.

SENTENCING

Gecht has always claimed innocence and managed to dodge the death sentence in court, receiving 120 years for his part in the attempted murder and rape of Beverley Washington.

B. 1953
LOCATION: USA
ALSO KNOWN AS:
"THE RIPPER CREW"
YEARS ACTIVE: 1982–83
MURDERS: 18

DAVID BERKOWITZ

N.Y.C. POLICE
4 176354
8 11 7 7

This indiscriminate New York murderer aspired to be as infamous as the serial killers he admired.

MEANS

The Bronx-raised Berkowitz was already familiar with minor crimes from his teenage years, obsessed as he was with setting fires and small acts of larceny. He enlisted in the US Army in 1971, going on to serve in the US and South Korea. Following his honourable discharge in 1974, he obtained an easily concealed but powerful .44-calibre Bulldog revolver that would become a key feature in the "Son of Sam" murders.

MOTIVE

Berkowitz was genetically inclined towards psychopathic tendencies, but his delicate psychological balance was probably tipped in his late teens or early twenties. He'd been adopted as an infant, and his adoptive mother died of cancer when he was 14. Upon returning from military service, Berkowitz located his birth mother and learned that he'd been illegitimate. This news crushed his fragile sense of identity, and was the catalyst for his alter ego the "Son of Sam", a man who aspired to the same notoriety that an as-yet unidentified serial killer on the other side of the country was enjoying – Ted Bundy.

OPPORTUNITY

Most of his crimes took place on dimly lit streets in the early evening or late at night, targeting young women and anyone who accompanied them. It was his style to ambush: survivors Donna DeMasi and Joanna Lomino describe a man in military fatigues approaching them and beginning to ask for directions before whipping out a handgun and firing rapidly at point-blank range.

CAPTURE

Berkowitz attacked Stacy Moskowitz and Robert Violante in July 1977 as they sat in a parked car. Witness Cacilia Davis spotted a man removing a parking ticket from his car moments after the attack – police checked all ticketed cars in the area, and the record included Berkowitz's yellow Ford Galaxie. It was traced to outside his apartment, where investigators spotted a rifle on the back seat. He was arrested as soon as he left his house and got into his car.

SENTENCING

Despite a bizarre effort to make investigators question his sanity (which included telling them that his neighbour's dog told him to kill), Berkowitz was declared sane and fit to stand trial. He got sentences of 25 years to life for each of the six murders of which he was convicted.

B. 1953
USA
ALSO KNOWN AS:
"THE SON OF SAM"
YEARS ACTIVE: 1976–77
MURDERS: 6

MICHAEL SWANGO

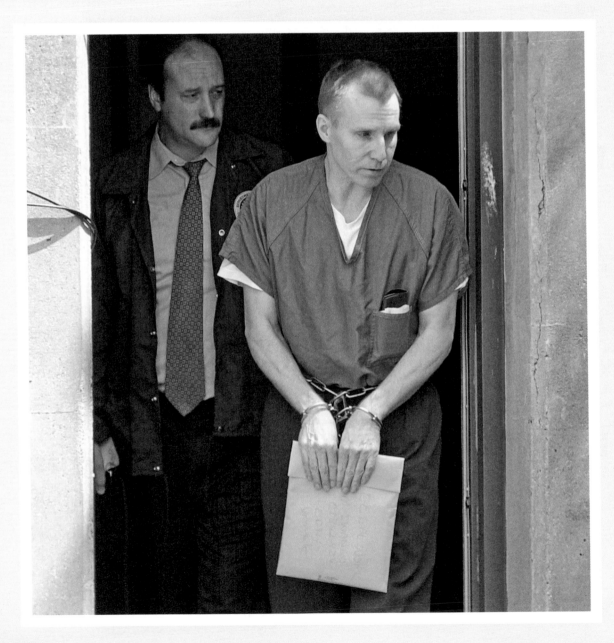

Washington-born Swango was a doctor with a dangerously developed god complex that led to murders in the US and Africa.

MEANS

Swango got a thrill out of poisoning patients, and anyone personally close to him, with deadly overdoses.

MOTIVE

He enjoyed the sense of power, of having his victims' lives in his hands. Long before he was suspected of poisoning, he had displayed a worrying obsession with the dying, shirking his studies at Southern Illinois University School of Medicine to focus on his work with emergency ambulance crews. At least five patients died on his watch.

OPPORTUNITY

Naturally, he had access to deadly poisons and prescription medicines. Several of his colleagues reported being violently ill after Swango had made them coffee on a break, and apparently healthy patients would suddenly die on wards he worked on in the Ohio State University Medical Center. His former girlfriend, a nurse called Kristin Kinney, said that her crippling migraines ceased once they split and she'd moved away.

CAPTURE

Swango never changed his methods. He was convicted once for poisoning his colleagues, given a five-year prison term and medically blacklisted. But he then fled to Zimbabwe and joined a mission hospital, where patients once again began to die mysteriously. Eventually, he was wanted by the Zimbabwean and US governments for several murders, so he pleaded guilty to charges of murder and fraud, to a US judge, to avoid the death penalty.

SENTENCING

He was given three life terms without the possibility of parole.

**B. 1954
LOCATION: USA
YEARS ACTIVE: 1981–97
MURDERS: 4+**

COLIN
IRELAND

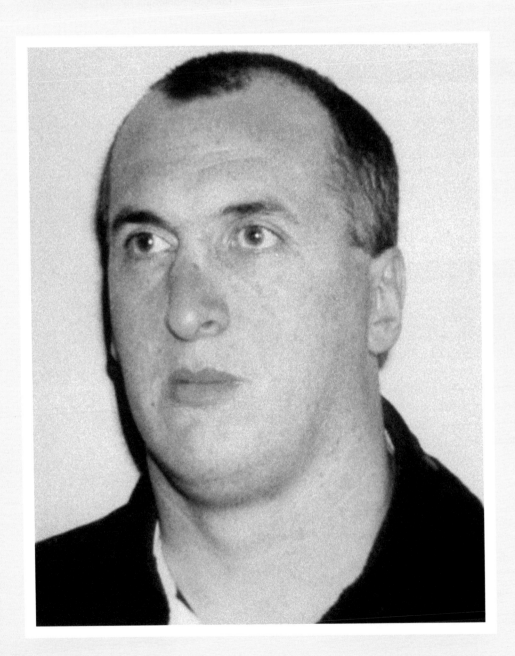

Ireland was responsible for the murders of several gay men he met in a bar in London, England.

MEANS

Ireland had a history of petty crimes in his youth and early adulthood. He also received some training in the British Army, which was probably where he picked up the organizational skills that featured in the execution of his murders. He made meticulous preparations for each victim and had a murder kit that comprised a knife, gloves and a change of clothing. He was a large man and his victims enjoyed being a submissive partner in sadomasochistic sex, so overpowering them was easy.

MOTIVE

He targeted homosexual men, whom he would accompany back to their homes. Ireland was married twice and claimed not to be homosexual himself. He certainly never got as far as having sex with his victims – once they had been willingly restrained, Ireland would reveal his true intentions for them and either strangle or asphyxiate the terrified men. He may well have been in denial of his true sexuality and murdering gay men was a symbolic way of killing an aspect of himself that he despised. The "reveal" was thrilling for Ireland; he enjoyed the brief time he had complete power over his victims.

OPPORTUNITY

Ireland would visit the Coleherne pub in west London, which at the time of his murders in 1993 was the go-to nightspot for "leather men" – homosexual men into bondage. He posed as a "top", or dominant partner, and let social engineering do the rest. Getting victims like Peter Walker and Emanuel Spiteri alone and bound was shockingly easy after that.

CAPTURE

CCTV captured Spiteri's last known movements, which were with Ireland. The killer made himself known to the police, who linked the other murders to him with forensic evidence from the crime scenes.

SENTENCING

He received life sentences for each of the five murder convictions.

**1954–2012
LOCATION: UK
DATES ACTIVE:
MARCH – JUNE 1993
ALSO KNOWN AS:
"THE GAY SLAYER"
MURDERS: 5**

KEITH HUNTER JESPERSON

Canadian-born trucker Jesperson killed women he met along his various routes. He became irate when a woman took credit for one of his murders.

MEANS

Keith Hunter Jesperson, also known as the "Happy Face Killer" after he scrawled a smiley face with confession to one of his murders in a public toilet, was a long-distance truck driver. This was his means of encountering the women he killed far from his Washington home and in at least one case, a method of disposing of the body: he strapped hitchhiker Angela Subrize to the undercarriage of his truck to grind her face away on the road, in the hope it would prevent police identifying her. Jesperson was a giant of a man who stood over two metres tall and manually strangled his victims, who would have been virtually powerless to stop him.

MOTIVE

Though Jesperson had a loving mother, his father was cruel and violent, and this influence might have put Jesperson on the road to his first murder, which he committed at the age of 35, when he had a wife and three children. He treated them all with the love a normal family man should – Jesperson was able to compartmentalize the "Happy Face Killer" so that his family didn't suspect a thing. In this way, he made the distinction between "good" women and the "trash" women he killed. Only after his arrest was his eldest daughter Melissa able to reflect on the rare occasions she saw glimmers of his dark side: when she was a child, he once killed a litter of kittens by hanging them from the washing line. And when she was older, Jesperson described his sex life with her mother in lurid detail, creating an intensely uncomfortable situation for his daughter.

OPPORTUNITY

Sex workers and trusting female hitchhikers were easy prey for a murderous trucker like Jesperson. It was socially conventional for them to approach his cab – then it was a simple case of pulling over at a quiet lay-by to commit rape and murder. In at least one case, he killed a woman (Taunja Bennett) he met at a bar after taking her back to his motel room.

CAPTURE

He almost confessed to his daughter, Melissa, just after he'd killed his seventh victim. Jesperson handed himself in after his eighth murder.

SENTENCING

He was given three consecutive life sentences.

**B. 1955
LOCATION: USA
ALSO KNOWN AS:
"THE HAPPY FACE KILLER"
YEARS ACTIVE: 1990–95
MURDERS: 8+**

JOE METHENY

Joe Metheny was a Maryland-born killer who claimed to have murdered three men and four women, boasting that he had taken cuts of their flesh and made them into burgers, selling them to the public on an "open pit beef stand".

MEANS

Two of the victims he claimed to have killed were homeless men, who he found passed out under a bridge in Baltimore, and hacked to death with an axe. He lured two sex workers to the same place and murdered them with his bare hands, then claimed to have beaten to death with a steel bar a man who was unfortunate enough to be fishing nearby. One of his confirmed victims, 26-year-old Kimberly Spicer, was stabbed to death, while 39-year-old Cathy Ann Magaziner was strangled and buried near the Joe Stein & Son pallet company, where Metheny worked as a forklift driver.

MOTIVE

Metheny claimed to have been neglected as a child after his father died when he was six and his mother had to work long hours to bring up her six children. But his mother refutes much of the blame her son pins on his upbringing, saying that extensive drug and alcohol abuse led to his murders. He eventually admitted to killing out of revenge against an ex-girlfriend, who he said took his son from him, and continued murdering simply because he "enjoyed it".

OPPORTUNITY

The two homeless men – for whose murders he was charged, but not convicted – he encountered when allegedly on his way to exact revenge against his ex. Metheny also used drugs to lure addicted female sex workers to secluded spots, like under the bridge.

CAPTURE

He was arrested in 1996 after the body of Kimberly Spicer was found underneath a trailer near his own.

SENTENCING

He was sentenced to death in 1997, though this was reduced to life imprisonment in 2000.

1955–2017
LOCATION: USA
YEARS ACTIVE: 1995–1996
MURDERS: 2+

AILEEN WUORNOS

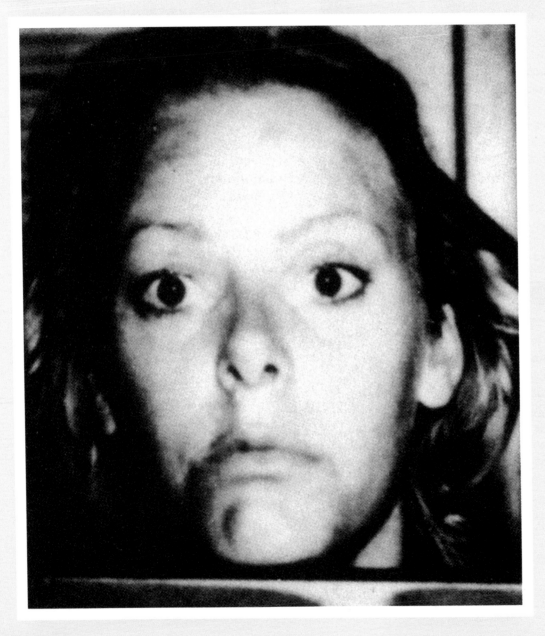

Much has been made of Wuornos in popular culture. Her murders, committed in the southern states, and the subsequent trial, captured international attention.

MEANS

Guns, cars and prostitution were a common theme in Wuornos's life. She owned a .22-calibre revolver and was turning tricks on the Florida highways at the time of the murders.

MOTIVE

On the face of it, it looks like Wuornos was simply killing and robbing her clients. Her childhood was far from well adjusted: she was abandoned by her mother, abused by her schizophrenic father (who committed suicide in jail), and beaten by her maternal grandfather. These early life experiences certainly would have damaged her psychological development. In these circumstances, she may have been unable to distinguish between interpersonal tension and someone who posed a genuine threat to her life. Perhaps Wuornos truly believed she killed in self defence? Three defense psychologists testified that she was psychologically impaired and was unable to conform to the law.

OPPORTUNITY

As a prostitute, Wuornos was easily able to lure her victims to her. These working-class, middle-aged family men had something to lose by being discovered with her, so they didn't need any convincing to find somewhere discreet to make their transaction. All Wuornos had to do once they reached a quiet stretch of road in the Florida backwaters was to produce her gun, order them out of the car and shoot them.

CAPTURE

Six months after the killer's palm print was taken off the handle of a vehicle she stole, police tracked her down to the now-infamous Last Resort bar in Volusia County, where they used her girlfriend to elicit a full confession from Wuornos.

SENTENCING

Wuornos was found guilty of six murders, sentenced to death and executed by lethal injection in 2002. Her strange last words were: "I'd just like to say I'm sailing with the rock, and I'll be back like *Independence Day* with Jesus June 6. Like the movie, big mother ship and all. I'll be back."

**1956–2002
LOCATION: USA
YEARS ACTIVE:
1989–1990
MURDERS: 6**

THE
LAST RESORT
BAR

LAST RESORT

The Last Resort biker bar in Port Orange, Florida. Aileen Wuornos was drinking a beer at the bar when she was apprehended and arrested on an outstanding warrant.

LUIS
GARAVITO

Garavito was a prolific child killer who, over a seven-year period, could have murdered more than any other known serial killer, if his full tally could ever be proven.

MEANS

He lured his young male victims with deception and treats, using sweets and sometimes disguising himself as a monk or an old man to win a child's trust. He tortured and killed his victims with knives or other sharp objects, easily overpowering them once he had led them away from public places.

MOTIVE

Garavito was a paedophile and a sexual sadist who took pleasure in the rape, prolonged torture and murder of children and teenagers. The judge assigned to the case described him as a psychopath, and the extreme nature of his crimes shows a complete lack of remorse.

OPPORTUNITY

Sadly, the state completely let Garavito's victims down. Political turmoil, corruption and the narcoterrorism of Colombia's civil war meant that mass graves and the bodies of murdered children were turning up with frightening frequency anyway. Garavito had his pick of Colombia's many poor and destitute children – waifs and strays who he didn't think would be missed – then literally buried them beneath bad news. Even worse, the country hadn't even conceived of an offence as extreme as his, so when he was caught, there was no provision in law to put such a dangerous criminal behind bars for his natural life.

CAPTURE

He was finally arrested for attempted rape on 22 April 1999.

SENTENCING

Garavito received a 1,853-year sentence. However, Colombia limits imprisonment to 40 years, and because of the deal he struck with police to reveal the location of the bodies, this was reduced to 22 years. He could be a free man by 2021.

**B.1957
LOCATION: COLOMBIA
YEARS ACTIVE:
1992–1999
MURDERS: 138+**

ÁNGEL MATURINO RESÉNDIZ

Mexican national Reséndiz hopped on and off freight trains to cross the US-Mexico border deep into the United States to where his victims were, and to beat a hasty retreat. He got his moniker after a pattern of grisly murders, bearing the hallmarks of the same killer, was discovered near the tracks.

MEANS

He would often use a blunt instrument found at the scene – a piece of plywood, a tyre iron or a pickaxe – to bludgeon his victims to death.

MOTIVE

Reséndiz would sometimes sexually assault his victims, but not always. He would sometimes steal cash and other valuables from the houses where he murdered people, but neither was financial gain his primary motive, and valuables would occasionally be left behind. Reséndiz at one point claimed to be an "angel of death", administering divine justice of sorts. His lawyer made an insanity plea, claiming that Reséndiz was a schizophrenic and was not eligible for the death penalty, but this wasn't successful.

OPPORTUNITY

He was an opportunistic serial killer and his victims' homes often had the ill fortune to lie along the path where he left the train track. As a physically small man, he had to rely on an ambush-style attack, often at night, breaking into houses and attacking victims as they slept. The attack on Christopher Maier and Holly Dunn Pendleton on a road near the tracks in Lexington, Kentucky, left Pendleton alive as the only known surviving witness to the Railroad Killer.

CAPTURE

His own sister finally handed him in, having seen his photo on an FBI Most Wanted poster, and convinced him to walk across the border into US custody.

SENTENCING

He was found guilty of capital murder and sentenced to death in 2000, and was executed by lethal injection in June 2006.

**1959–2006
LOCATION: USA
ALSO KNOWN AS:
"THE RAILROAD KILLER"
YEARS ACTIVE: 1986–1999
MURDERS: 15+**

MAJID SALEK MOHAMMADI

Not long after the 1979 Iranian Revolution, Mohammadi embarked on a spree of violent attacks on women in and around Tehran, which became known as the "White Rope Murders".

MEANS

Mohammadi drove a green Chevrolet and used a length of white rope to strangle all of his victims. He also had an ID card that he used in at least one of his murders to convince the victim that he was her driver and she should get into his car.

MOTIVE

One of the case investigators thought Mohammadi chose victims he believed were being unfaithful to their husbands. It may be more than just coincidence that he began murdering women shortly after the Islamic Republic had been established, perhaps feeling tacit support for his crimes from the state, which had gone about actively removing women's rights. This doesn't fully explain why Mohammadi also murdered the children found with some of the women.

OPPORTUNITY

Mohammadi would seek victims by driving around Tehran and the nearby village of Evin.

CAPTURE

His final victim's sister witnessed a slim man in his 30s with dark skin and an Azebaijani accent picking her up in his green Chevrolet, after which she was never seen alive again. Mohammadi was arrested on 24 February 1985, after driving around in search of another woman to kill.

SENTENCING

Mohammadi committed suicide in his cell before he could face sentencing.

**UNKNOWN–1985
LOCATION: IRAN
YEARS ACTIVE: 1981–1985
MURDERS: 24**

JEFFREY
LIONEL DAHMER

POLICE DEPT   BATH, OH
0·07·81
81 120

Cannibal killer Jeffrey Dahmer was a loner who targeted boys and gay men, storing their body parts in his flat.

MEANS

When police in Milwaukee, Wisconsin, raided Dahmer's apartment on 924 North 25th Street, they didn't have to look hard to find evidence that he had the tools to both murder and dispose of bodies. Dahmer wasn't exactly discreet: the stench of the dissolving bodies he kept in a 57-gallon drum in his room was seeping into the corridor outside. He kept a sharp hunting knife under his mattress as well as a pair of handcuffs. He also had a fridge, which is where the cops found some of the most incriminating evidence – various limbs and organs belonging to some of the many men he'd brought home.

MOTIVE

Though he was deemed to be legally sane at his trial, he was diagnosed with several psychological disorders. At least one would-be victim who escaped from Apartment 213, Tracy Edwards, noted Dahmer's strange behaviour, which included rocking back and forth, chanting and then telling Edwards that he was going to eat his heart. But Dahmer was generally lucid enough to understand what compelled him to murder, to experiment on the bodies of his victims in Frankensteinian ways, to cannibalize their flesh and to build a macabre shrine out of their bones: it was all about control. More specifically, he did this to wholly possess these men and prevent them from ever leaving. It was "the only motive there ever was", he later admitted in an NBC interview.

OPPORTUNITY

As a young, fit and handsome gay man, Dahmer had little trouble engaging men at Milwaukee's gay bars and enticing them back to his apartment. They would readily drink alcoholic beverages laced with sleeping pills, like 25-year-old Raymond Smith, or relax enough to drop their guard, at which point Dahmer would snap handcuffs onto their wrists, as in the case of Tracy Edwards.

CAPTURE

Edwards managed to escape from Dahmer's home and he immediately informed the police, who were horrified by what they subsequently found there.

SENTENCING

He was convicted of 16 murders and sentenced to a life term for each, though he was himself murdered in prison just two years after the trial.

**1960–94
ALSO KNOWN AS:
"THE MILWAUKEE
CANNIBAL"
LOCATION: USA
YEARS ACTIVE: 1978–91
MURDERS: 17**

RICARDO LEYVA MUÑOZ "RICHARD" RAMÍREZ

Californian killer Richard Ramírez would case suburban homes before breaking in and murdering the occupants.

MEANS

As a boy, Ramírez regularly enjoyed hunting trips with his family, in which he practised sneaking up to animals and stabbing them. In his teens, he would break into and enter houses with his elder brother Ruben, a more experienced burglar who showed him how to gain access to and explore private properties undetected. Ramírez later employed these learned skills in his horrific campaign of violence. He armed himself before each of his crimes, though he was capable of making a weapon out of anything that came to hand. He was familiar enough with the Californian homes he broke into to know where guns or knives were likely to be stashed.

MOTIVE

Sex and violence merged for Ramírez at a young age, with experiences and injury likely playing a pivotal role in his pathology. His mother's job in a shoe factory exposed him to chemicals in utero and he suffered a serious head injury at five years old. His cousin Mike, on his return from the Vietnam War, showed a 12-year-old Ramírez photos of Vietnamese women he'd raped and murdered, and a year later, fatally shot his wife in the face while Ramírez looked on. This made an indelible impression on the boy's fragile mind. From that point on, Ramírez steadily descended into a life of drug abuse and crime.

OPPORTUNITY

After his fifth and sixth murders, of Vincent Zazzara and his wife Maxine, Ramírez established a modus operandi in which he would immediately kill the male occupant of the house before he sexually assaulted and murdered their female partner. The homes he broke into were often selected from quiet, dark and unsecured streets.

CAPTURE

After tracing fingerprints left at a crime scene to Ramírez's lengthy rap sheet, police supplied a mugshot to the press, which Ramírez saw on a newspaper rack. He fled in a panic but was quickly apprehended by bystanders who recognized him.

SENTENCING

He was found guilty of 13 counts of murder and sentenced to death, but died of cancer on death row 23 years later.

**1960–2013
LOCATION: USA
YEARS ACTIVE:
1984–85
ALSO KNOWN AS: "THE
NIGHT STALKER"
MURDERS: 14**

Ramírez surrounded by police and with his hands cuffed behind his back, August 1985.

JOHN ALLEN
MUHAMMAD

Former US Army engineer Muhammad was the older of the two perpetrators of the Washington sniper attacks in 2002, and arguably the brains behind the abhorrent crime.

MEANS

Muhammad bought a decommissioned police car, a blue Chevrolet Caprice, and modified it so he could lie flat across the back seats and point his Bushmaster rifle through a hole in the boot. He and his accomplice, Lee Boyd Malvo, were able to discreetly target and shoot people at random in the 2002 Washington Beltway sniper attacks in and around the American capital.

MOTIVE

A clear motive was never established for the sniper attacks. Muhammad's ex-wife Mildred claimed that the apparently random murders were a smokescreen for an attempt on her life, and his planned revenge for her taking the children away from him. It seemed Muhammad acquired a taste for the power of choosing life or death for the unwitting members of the public who walked into the crosshairs of his rifle; on numerous occasions, he told the police to call him "God" via anonymous phone calls and on a calling card left at the scene of 13-year-old Iran Brown's shooting. Muhammad also wrote of waging "jihad" against the United States and sympathizing with the terrorist group al-Qaeda, though terrorism was largely dismissed by most courts (except one in Virginia) as a motive.

OPPORTUNITY

In the wake of the arrest, investigators were able to establish that Muhammad had invested a great deal of planning into each shooting. He was easily able to place himself at the scene of each shooting without arousing suspicion, especially at the start of the killing spree, before the murders had been linked to his vehicle.

CAPTURE

After police found a rifle magazine bearing Malvo's fingerprints at the scene of one of the pair's final shootings, they were able to link him to Muhammad. Police caught Muhammad red-handed, asleep in his car with the rifle in the back, on 24 October 2002.

SENTENCING

Muhammad was sentenced to death for capital murder in 2009 and executed the same year.

1960–2009
LOCATION: USA
DATES ACTIVE: 2002
MURDERS: 17

SÜLEYMAN AKTAŞ

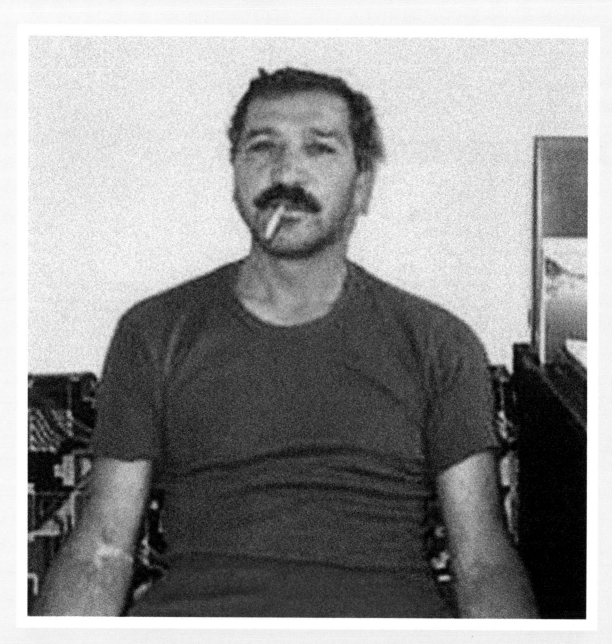

A father of two, Aktaş was known as "The Nailing Killer" after murdering four elderly people in Çambaşı village, southwest Turkey, in 1994, and a police captain in 1986.

MEANS

He beat two of his victims unconscious with a hammer and manually strangled all of them. He also used a nail gun to shoot nails into their faces.

MOTIVE

Aktaş was an electrical engineer who was working on a high-voltage line in 1986 when he was electrocuted with 31,500 volts. He survived after a period of intensive care, but the accident had damaged him psychologically. He was diagnosed with paranoid schizophrenia, telling doctors that he was ordered by the authorities to kill, that he couldn't stand nails and that he had to stop his victims from seeing them.

OPPORTUNITY

Not long after he recovered from his accident, Aktaş murdered a policeman, Captain Nuri Keskin in Antalya. His final four victims – Ayşe Güneş and her husband İsmail and Rukiye Kocatepe and her husband Ramazan – were his neighbours when he moved back to his village in 1990.

CAPTURE

After the murder of the Kocatepes, Aktaş told his relatives what he had done, who informed the police. He was arrested in 1994 and made a full confession. Police found a list in Aktaş's flat of the people he intended to murder, who lived below him in the same building.

SENTENCING

He was returned to Manisa Mental and Diseases Hospital for treatment. Today, he insists he will continue his "mission" if he is released.

**B.1960, ESTIMATED
LOCATION: TURKEY
YEARS ACTIVE:
1986–1994
MURDERS: 5**

GUY
GEORGES

This rapist and murderer preyed on attractive young female victims who were mostly attacked in the historic eastern quarter of Paris.

MEANS

Georges would sexually assault them and then use a knife to either stab or slit their throats, or strangle them with his bare hands.

MOTIVE

He was a foster child whose adoptive parents were simply unable to give him the love a child needed, returning him to the authorities at the age of 16 after he attacked two of his foster sisters. At his 2001 trial, the psychiatrists who assessed his mental fitness to stand trial deemed him a narcissistic psychopath. Whatever dark passions drove him to sexual violence were matched by a morbid interest in his dying victims: he admitted to watching 19-year-old Pascale Escarfail bleed to death from the awful wound he'd inflicted on her throat. By contrast, he was far from a repellant misanthrope in the squats on Rue Didot in the 15th arrondissement, where he lived. He was well liked by other squatters and even had a girlfriend.

OPPORTUNITY

From the age of 19, Georges began a campaign of rape and violent assault on women that nearly always ended in him stabbing, sometimes killing them. He would follow his intended victims to their homes, where he would strike. Catherine Rocher was murdered in an underground car park in January 1994, as was Elsa Benady in November that same year. Like Pascale Escarfail, he managed to gain entry to Helena Frinking's apartment, where she was murdered in July 1995.

CAPTURE

After seven years and as many murder victims, Georges was caught on 26 March 1998 after police matched his DNA to suspect DNA found at four of the crime scenes.

SENTENCING

He was given a life sentence in 2001, with no possibility of parole before 2023.

**B.1962
LOCATION: FRANCE
ALSO KNOWN AS:
"THE BEAST OF THE
BASTILLE"
1991–1997
MURDERS: 7**

DIMITRIS VAKRINOS

Vakrinos was a taxi driver who lived in the Moschato suburb of Athens, in the south of the country, for most of his life. His victims were killed for perceived slights or injustices.

MEANS

He killed a guest in his house, Panayiotis Gaglias, with an iron bar as he slept. Others he shot and one, Anastasia Simitzi, he doused in petrol and burned alive. He used his own taxi as transport to and from the scene for some of the crimes.

MOTIVE

Vakrinos had an acute inferiority complex and these crimes were thought to be a grossly disproportionate means of answering challenges: Gaglias threatened to tell police that Vakrinos had stolen his gun, and Simitzi spurned his overt advances when she climbed into his taxi after a night out. Two of his survivors, teenagers Andrea Svyrus and Theodoros Bitoulas, were shot simply because they had made derogatory comments about a couple out for a walk, which Vakrinos had overheard.

OPPORTUNITY

As a taxi driver, he knew or had some professional contact with some of his victims. He was also a thief. The legal owners of property he had stolen challenged him, and his reaction was to kill. Case in point, the murders of brothers Kostas and Antonis Spyropoulos, whose car Vakrinos had stolen.

CAPTURE

He was arrested in April 1997, but committed suicide in jail before he could be sentenced.

1962–1997
LOCATION: GREECE
YEARS ACTIVE: 1987–1996
MURDERS: 5

TSUTOMU MIYAZAKI

Miyazaki was an extremely disturbed paedophile who murdered primary school girls in and around the city of Tokyo, drank their blood and engaged in various necrophilic acts. The killer was distinguished by his obsession with extreme manga and anime, and his trial caused a moral panic in Japan.

MEANS

He used a vehicle to cruise around and select a victim at random, and a camera to take photos of them and various items on their person. He posted a box containing photographs of four-year-old Mari Konno's shorts, 10 baby teeth and charred remains to her family. He taunted the families of each of his victims with postcards featuring the girls' names and words like "death" and "bones", formed by letters clipped from magazines.

MOTIVE

Miyazaki was born with a defect that left him with deformed hands and made him a target for bullies at school. He threw himself into a fantasy world of manga comics and, later, child pornography. The murders were the culmination of his extreme fantasies, and at his trial he was diagnosed with schizophrenia.

OPPORTUNITY

The oldest of his victims, Masami Yoshizawa, was seven years old when he passed her on a road in

Hanno, just north of Tokyo. Like his other victims before and after her, Yoshizawa was easily convinced to get into the car by Miyazaki.

CAPTURE

He was finally captured after he separated a young girl from her sister and began to take nude photos of her. The older sister ran home and told her parents, who called the police after accosting Miyazaki. He was arrested on 23 July 1989.

SENTENCING

He was given a death sentence and was executed by hanging in 2008.

**1962–2008
LOCATION: JAPAN
YEARS ACTIVE: 1988–1989
MURDERS: 4**

ADOLFO CONSTANZO

As the leader of a bloody Mexican cult based near Mexico City, Constanzo kidnapped and butchered victims with the help of his followers, requiring a live human sacrifice for his spells.

MEANS

A machete was commonly used to kill his victims, dismember their corpses and to retrieve body parts, including their brains. A red pickup truck was used in the abduction of at least one of the victims, American student Mark Kilroy, and an iron cauldron was used to boil body parts for the cult's potions. Many of the murders took place at a desert ranch around 100 miles from Mexico City.

MOTIVE

Constanzo was drawn into a dark Afro-Cuban cult called Palo Mayombe as a teenager, which is when he began ritual animal sacrifice. This escalated once he moved to Mexico City, where he gathered followers. He found that dealers from powerful local drug cartels were attracted to the bloodletting rituals his cult offered. They could easily afford the many thousands of dollars he charged to weave them spells and charms that would allow their illicit deals to go smoothly. As demand increased for his services, the stakes rose. Eventually, Constanzo decided that his spell potions – forged in a "nganga", or cauldron – required a fresh human brain.

OPPORTUNITY

He took advantage of the political and social chaos in Mexico City to pick off low-level dealers and enemies of his clients as the source of human brains for his potion. But when Constanzo decided he needed a quality brain of an American student, he waited until thousands of "spring breakers" descended on the coastal border city of Matamoros. 21-year-old University of Texas student Mark Kilroy was simply in the wrong place at the wrong time that evening of 14 March 1989: he was dragged into a red pickup by Constanzo's henchmen and driven to the ranch where he was tortured and beheaded.

DEATH

When Mark Kilroy's parents reported their son missing, it sparked a huge search by US and Mexican forces that ended with his remains, along with those of at least 14 others, being dug up at Rancho Santa Elena. Constanzo fled to Mexico City, but later ordered one of his henchmen to shoot him dead when police closed in on him.

**1962–1989
LOCATION: MEXICO
YEARS ACTIVE:
1986–1989
MURDERS: 23+**

CHRISTINE FALLING

Sadly, far too many parents entrusted their young children to this deadly Floridian babysitter.

MEANS

As a teenager, Christine Falling liked to kill small animals, especially cats, which she dropped from several storeys to "test their nine lives". She later suffered from hallucinations and was hospitalized. Following her release from hospital, she worked as a babysitter for family and friends in her Florida hometown, which is when babies in her care began to die.

MOTIVE

Epilepsy and mental illness drove Falling to kill. When confronted by police, she immediately confessed to hearing voices that told her to kill each infant. She was also a deeply insecure person, and killing babies briefly put the power of life and death into her hands.

OPPORTUNITY

As a trusted babysitter, Falling was given the responsibility of toddlers and babies as young as 10 weeks, as in the case of Travis Coleman. When left alone, she would find an opportunity to smother them. She also worked in a nursing home for elderly people for a while, during which time 77-year-old William Swindle died. A catalogue of medical errors meant she got away with the first five murders, which were invariably misdiagnosed as sudden infant death syndrome or a viral infection.

CAPTURE

Doctors finally recognized signs of manual suffocation in the autopsy of Travis Coleman, after which Falling was arrested.

SENTENCING

She was sentenced to life imprisonment with a minimum term of 25 years. Her parole was rejected in 2017.

B. 1963
LOCATION: USA
YEARS ACTIVE: 1980–82
MURDERS: 6

RUSSELL WILLIAMS

Williams was a highly decorated colonel in the Royal Canadian Air Force who led a double life, raping and murdering women near his home and Canadian Forces Base Trenton in Ontario.

MEANS

The two women he was convicted of murdering were beaten unconscious with a flashlight and bound with gaffer tape or rope. He photographed and videotaped his victims as he sexually assaulted them. He suffocated Marie-France Comeau with gaffer tape and strangled Jessica Lloyd with a rope.

MOTIVE

Williams's specific sexual motive began with a fetish for breaking into houses and stealing women's (and sometimes young girls') underwear, which escalated over four years and over 100 break-ins to rape, then murder.

OPPORTUNITY

Thirty-seven-year-old Marie-France Comeau was a corporal at CFB Trenton and known to Williams. He broke into her house in November 2009 and waited in the basement until she came home and went to bed, then ambushed her. On the evening of 28 January 2010, Williams drove to 27-year-old Jessica Lloyd's house in his Nissan Pathfinder SUV, having noticed her on her treadmill as he'd passed on the road earlier. He waited in the bushes before breaking in. After subjecting her to a three-hour ordeal, he drove her to his cottage nearby and murdered her.

CAPTURE

After a police officer noticed the similarity of the tyre treads of Williams's SUV to the imprint of the vehicle left outside Jessica Lloyd's house, Williams was brought in for questioning and then arrested on 8 February 2010. He made a full confession.

SENTENCING

He was stripped of his rank and given two concurrent life sentences.

**B.1963
LOCATION: CANADA
ALSO KNOWN AS:
"THE KILLER COLONEL"
YEARS ACTIVE: 2009–2010
MURDERS: 2+**

DOMINIQUE COTTREZ

Over the course of 17 years, Cottrez murdered at least eight of her own newborn children. She buried two in the garden of her first address in Villers-au-Tertre, northern France, and hid six in a fuel tank in the garage of her second address in the same town.

MEANS

Cottrez smothered each infant shortly after they were born, with a cushion or her bare hands. She placed each tiny corpse in a plastic bag.

MOTIVE

Mr and Mrs Cottrez were considered a quiet and respectable couple in their town, but this masked Dominique's deep psychological problems. Postnatal depression was considered for motive in her case. The prosecution later told the press, "[S]he did not want any more children and … she did not want to see a doctor about methods of contraception."

OPPORTUNITY

Cottrez was able to disguise her pregnancies from her husband, even in their later stages, because she was clinically obese.

CAPTURE

She was arrested after the skeletons of the first two children she killed were found by the new owners of her old property, while digging in the garden. She immediately confessed to the two murders and six more.

SENTENCING

Cottrez was convicted of eight murders and sentenced – mitigating circumstances considered – to nine years' imprisonment in 2015. She served three and was released in 2018.

B.1964
LOCATION: FRANCE
YEARS ACTIVE:
1989–2006
MURDERS: 8

PAUL BERNARDO

Scarborough-born Bernardo was from a middle-class family, marrying Karla Homolka in 1991 and progressing from violent rape to murder with her assistance. One of his victims was Homolka's younger sister Tammy.

MEANS

Bernardo was a serial rapist in his hometown long before his first murder. He used a knife to threaten these victims into submission. Two of his murder victims, Lesley Mahaffy and Tammy Homolka, were given fatal doses of sedatives his wife obtained from the veterinary clinic where she worked. Kristen French was strangled with a cord tied to a hope chest. He made videos and took photos of some of the assaults.

MOTIVE

After being brought up by an abusive father, Bernardo had developed dark sexual fantasies by his teens. He sought complete control over women and enjoyed humiliating them in public, including his own mother. By the time he met Homolka, he was looking for a virgin to abuse, a desire she helped him fulfil. Leslie Mahaffy and Kristen French were killed to keep them from identifying Bernardo. A psychiatric assessment for his trial found that Bernardo scored highly on the psychopathy checklist, used in professional assessment.

OPPORTUNITY

Leslie Mahaffy was forced into Bernardo's car after he passed her while she was outside her house, having been locked out. Kristen French was dragged into his car as she walked home from school, after Homolka pretended to ask for directions. Tammy Homolka was drugged with a spiked drink in the basement of her own home.

CAPTURE

Bernardo was initially arrested in connection with the Scarborough rapes in 1993, and eventually connected to the murders after Karla Homolka made a plea deal.

SENTENCING

In 1995, Bernardo was sentenced to life imprisonment, and 25 years without the chance of parole.

**B.1964
LOCATION: CANADA
YEARS ACTIVE:
1986–1992
MURDERS: 3+**

GAO CHENGYONG

Gao Chengyong targeted women wearing red in northern parts of China and Inner Mongolia, taking body parts and organs as souvenirs.

MEANS

Gao thoroughly deserved his moniker, the "Chinese Jack the Ripper". He used a blade to stab and slash his victims' throats and mutilate their bodies, dismembering and removing the reproductive organs of some of the women he killed.

MOTIVE

Broadly speaking, the murders were sexually driven. All his victims were wearing red, which is thought to have some significance in interpreting sexual readiness, and all were raped prior to being murdered. In the original Jack the Ripper case, some experts think the mutilation of the bodies was a form of humiliating the victim, exposing them in the most graphic way imaginable. That could also have played a part in Gao's murders.

OPPORTUNITY

Gao targeted lone women, often following them home. At least one victim came into his shop in the village of Baiyin, in northwest China. He also knew enough about the women he murdered to know that they lived alone.

CAPTURE

The murders stopped in 2002 and the case went cold until 2015, when a strong familial link was made between the murderer's DNA and Gao's uncle, who had been arrested for a minor offence. A simple process of elimination then led police to arrest Gao in August 2016.

SENTENCING

He was sentenced to death in 2018 and executed in January 2019.

**1964–2019
LOCATION: PEOPLE'S
REPUBLIC OF CHINA
ALSO KNOWN AS:
"CHINESE JACK
THE RIPPER"
DATES ACTIVE:
1998–2002
MURDERS: 11**

MOSES SITHOLE

Sithole is South Africa's most prolific known serial killer, raping and murdering women in Atteridgeville, then Boksburg and Cleveland, which led to his moniker.

MEANS

He overpowered and beat his victims with his bare hands, bound them with their own clothing and then strangled them with their underwear.

MOTIVE

After his release from prison in 1993, following time served for a rape conviction, Sithole began his serial murders in earnest. In an anonymous phone call to a newspaper, *The Star*, he claimed that he raped and murdered in retaliation for the previous sentence he received for crimes he didn't commit. Power and control were his motives for murder.

OPPORTUNITY

Sithole would dress and pose as a businessman and offer young women work for a charity he had set up. Once he gained their trust, he would lead them away from the town across the grassland to "his office". When he felt they were at a safe distance, he would attack.

CAPTURE

The same day Sithole had phoned the newspaper, police traced several job applications some of the victims had made to Sithole. As the net closed, Sithole went on the run and contacted his brother-in-law, asking for a gun. Instead, his brother-in-law called the police, who arrested him.

SENTENCING

He was found guilty of 38 murders, and sentenced to a total of 2,410 years' imprisonment.

**B.1964
LOCATION:
SOUTH AFRICA
ALSO KNOWN AS:
"THE ABC KILLER"
YEARS ACTIVE:
1994–1995
MURDERS: 38+**

JOHN
BUNTING

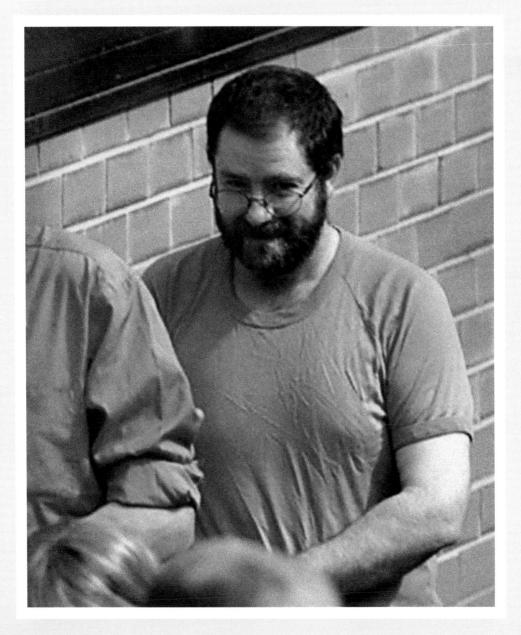

Bunting was the ringleader of a group of vigilante torture-murderers from Adelaide, South Australia. They targeted people who either were homosexual or were paedophiles, or were suspected of being so by Bunting.

MEANS

He had made a "rock spider" (a slang term for a paedophile) wall chart, similar to what you might see in a police investigation room, to keep track of potential targets. He beat one of his victims to death with a shovel, another with a cudgel, and others through manual strangulation or using cord. His later murders involved electrocuting his victims with a metallurgy tool attached to their skin via alligator clips. He dismembered eight of the bodies with a saw and put them in six plastic barrels filled with hydrochloric acid, leaving them in an old bank vault he and his accomplices rented in Snowtown, nearly 100 miles north of Adelaide.

MOTIVE

Bunting and his main accomplices, Robert Wagner and James Vlassakis, stole money and welfare cheques amounting to many thousands of dollars from their victims. But according to British psychiatrist Professor Kevin Howells, Bunting's motive was to have complete control over his victims; Howells concluded that Bunting was a psychopath with no empathy and a lack of emotion.

OPPORTUNITY

All but one of Bunting's victims were either neighbours or someone he or one of his accomplices otherwise knew personally. Two were James Vlassakis's half brothers. One, Gary O'Dwyer, was a complete stranger.

CAPTURE

After eight of his victims were discovered in the Snowtown bank vault and two more in a shallow grave in Bunting's former home in Adelaide, Bunting was arrested.

SENTENCING

In 2003, Bunting was found guilty of 11 murders and given 11 consecutive life sentences.

**B.1966
LOCATION:
AUSTRALIA
YEARS ACTIVE:
1992–1999
MURDERS: 11**

JOSÉ VICENTE MATIAS

Matias was a cannibal who heard disembodied voices, killing his female victims in the name of the devil.

MEANS

This cannibal killer had a considerable size and strength advantage against the women he targeted, dispatching his six known victims with sticks or stones he'd found on the beach or, in one case, with a knife.

MOTIVE

He drank the blood and consumed parts of his victims' brain matter, telling the police that the devil had "whispered in his ear" and told him to kill seven women. Three of his victims were tourists or immigrants, and he also told the police that he hated the way foreigners came to his country to mock Brazilians. Either way, there was no doubt that Matias was mentally unhinged. Rape certainly featured in some of the murders, although Matias was impotent. The resulting frustration and shame might have driven him to kill.

OPPORTUNITY

Matias was a charming man on the surface and in at least two of the murders, that of 29-year-old Russian tourist Katrya Ratikov and 27-year-old Spanish tourist Nuria Fernández Collada, he was able to convince them to walk with him to lonely places – into the countryside and to a remote

CAPTURE

After six years and at least as many murder victims, he was arrested in March 2005.

SENTENCING

On 2 June 2008, Matias was sentenced to 23 years in prison.

**B.1966
BRAZIL
ALSO KNOWN AS:
"CORUMBÁ"
DATES ACTIVE: 1999–2005
MURDERS: 6**

HERIBERTO SEDA

For a few years in the early 90s, copycat killer Heriberto Seda murdered indiscriminately in New York City

MEANS

Seda was able to craft himself a zip gun (a kind of homemade gang pistol that uses real bullets) to prevent police from identifying his weapon. He killed, or attempted murder, whenever there was a certain constellation in the sky, and taunted New York City police with cryptic, coded messages.

MOTIVE

Seda was a copycat killer, who aspired to be as infamous as the still-unidentified Zodiac Killer who terrorized California in the 1960s and 1970s. Seda may have used his Zodiac copycat persona to justify his violent urges and lose his inhibitions. For a while, police considered the possibility that this was the original Zodiac Killer, relocated to the east of the country.

OPPORTUNITY

His victims were shot or stabbed seemingly at random, most after Seda had caught them unawares on the street in New York. He planned to kill 12 – one for each sign of the Zodiac – before ceasing his murders, like the Zodiac Killer.

CAPTURE

He made the mistake of pulling a gun on his half-sister and her boyfriend, after which the police were called. They didn't link this case to the murders until they saw his written statement: it contained a symbol that looked very similar to the ones used on the taunts the NYPD had received. Seda's matching DNA was subsequently found on a stamp used to mail one of the killer's letters.

SENTENCING

After a six-week trial, Seda was found guilty of three murders and one attempted murder. He was sentenced to a total of 232 years in prison.

B.1967
LOCATION: USA
YEARS ACTIVE: 1990–93
ALSO KNOWN AS:
ZODIAC (COPYCAT)
MURDERS: 3

PETR ZELENKA

Zelenka was the head nurse of an intensive-care unit in a hospital in Havlíčkův Brod, southern Czech Republic. Over a five-month period, he killed seven patients and attempted to murder 10 more.

MEANS

As a nurse, Zelenka had access to vital medicines. He injected his victims with fatal doses of the blood-thinning drug, heparin.

MOTIVE

Zelenka tried unsuccessfully to plead insanity at his trial, claiming that he wasn't in control of his actions and that a "voice" told him to inject patients on his ward. "The first impulse to kill came out of nowhere … I had a feeling that someone was trying to persuade me to do it." But his actual motive became clearer in an afterthought, when he tried to explain to the court why he chose the drug, heparin: "I knew the patients would suffer from internal bleeding but I thought we would try to save their lives. I did not intend to kill them. I just wanted some action. I enjoyed the work."

OPPORTUNITY

The murders began when Zelenka was promoted to head nurse. Naturally, a great deal of trust was placed in him to care for his patients appropriately, many of whom were unconscious or unresponsive and in no position to refuse treatment or bear witness to his crimes.

CAPTURE

After head doctor Pavel Longin noticed that an unusually large number of patients were bleeding to death on Zelenka's ward, and that Zelenka was the last person to treat them, the nurse was dismissed. He was arrested in December of the same year.

SENTENCING

He was given a life term in a maximum security prison for the murders, although Judge Jiří Vacek pulled no punches in sentencing, saying that if capital punishment were still available to him, he would have given Zelenka the death penalty.

**B.1976
LOCATION: CZECH
REPUBLIC
YEARS ACTIVE: 2006
MURDERS: 7**

YAVUZ YAPICIOĞLU

Responsible for a series of fatal stabbings around Istanbul and northwestern Turkey that earned him his moniker, Yapıcıoğlu is thought to have killed many more than he was convicted of – enough to make him Turkey's most prolific murderer.

MEANS

He used a screwdriver to stab many of his known victims, as well as a knife and a heavy crystal ashtray.

MOTIVE

Yapıcıoğlu had a history of explosive, unpredictable violence and arson, long before he first killed. And when he did kill, it was often for the most inconsequential of reasons. So, even in between the murders, there was some dispute over his sanity: Bakırköy Psychiatric Hospital in Istanbul determined that Yapıcıoğlu had diminished responsibility in the murders, though a court-ordered examination in 2002 essentially said he was faking it. Yapıcıoğlu told that court that he sometimes lost his sense of time and where he was, and that the murders had taken place during these times.

OPPORTUNITY

His victims were mostly strangers: three people stabbed to death in Istanbul in 1994 after one of them greeted him, two more on a coach that had stopped in Ankara, and three more in the city of Çorlu. His grandmother died after he smashed an ashtray on her head when she told him something he didn't like about his mother, and he attempted to kill his father, too.

CAPTURE

He was arrested for the final time on Christmas Eve 2002.

SENTENCING

Yapıcıoğlu was deemed sane and fully liable for his crimes in 2003, and sentenced to life in Tekirdağ Prison, eastern Turkey.

B.1967
LOCATION: TURKEY
ALSO KNOWN AS:
"THE SCREWDRIVER
KILLER"
YEARS ACTIVE: 1994–2002
MURDERS: 18+

BEVERLEY ALLITT

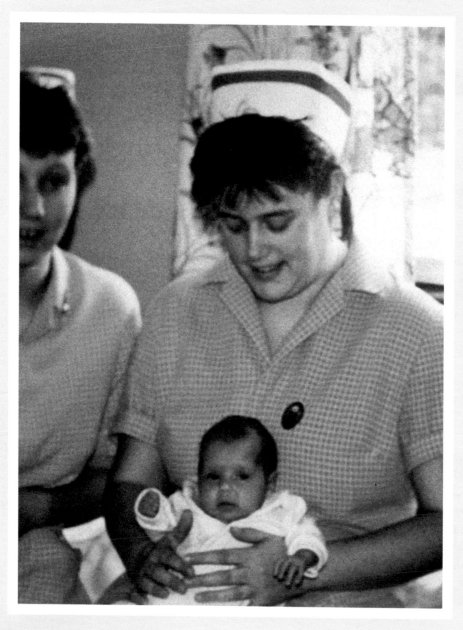

English nurse Beverley Allitt poisoned young children in her care to gain the attention that she craved.

MEANS

Working as a nurse in a ward at Grantham and Kesteven Hospital in England, Beverley Allitt was responsible for many sick children. She had access to the locked refrigerator that contained insulin and, at the time of her first murder, she was the last person known to have been in possession of the key. Her victims stopped breathing after slipping into a coma brought on by hypoglycaemia – a result of the insulin Allitt had administered.

MOTIVE

Allitt had a condition called Munchausen syndrome by proxy, a psychological disorder in which a person fakes or induces symptoms in another person. In Allitt's case, she craved the attention of parents and hospital staff that she got whenever a child in her care fell ill. Five-month-old Paul Crampton's parents trusted Allitt with one-to-one care of their child and even brought her with them in the ambulance after the third time he suffered a hypoglycaemic attack.

OPPORTUNITY

The hospital was severely understaffed and on each and every occasion that a child fell sick in Allitt's care, Allitt had been left alone with the child. Two-month-old Becky Phillips had been discharged from hospital, but her parents took Allitt home with them to help with close monitoring, which proved to be a fatal mistake.

CAPTURE

Staff suspected that someone was deliberately poisoning children at the hospital, but they weren't able to pinpoint who it was and arrest Allitt until they plotted nurse shift patterns against the times children were collapsing.

SENTENCING

Allitt denied all charges but was found guilty of four counts of murder, five counts of attempted murder and six counts of grievous bodily harm. She was given 13 life sentences.

B.1968
LOCATION: UK
YEARS ACTIVE: FEBRUARY–APRIL 1991
ALSO KNOWN AS: "THE ANGEL OF DEATH"
MURDERS: 4

LEVI
BELLFIELD

Levi Bellfield was a narcissistic killer who mainly targeted young girls in South East England, approaching them in a vehicle and attacking them when they refused his advances.

MEANS

Bellfield's modus operandi was to approach lone women and bludgeon his victim over the head with a heavy instrument, run them over in his vehicle, or a combination of the two. He ran a wheel-clamping business in west London, so he routinely kept heavy tools in his van.

MOTIVE

He had a history of committing petty crimes, and all of the women with whom he had a relationship told a similar story: that Bellfield was charming at first but then he quickly became abusive and controlling. Investigators characterized his attacks as being partly borne out of his massive ego. A perceived snub from the women or young girls he approached would elicit incandescent rage, which led an indignant Bellfield to murder the "worthless" subject of his unwanted advances. Since Bellfield's imprisonment, a 2017 report has emerged that links him to a London paedophile ring.

OPPORTUNITY

Bellfield would typically trawl the streets looking for a vulnerable young woman. In the investigation of Bellfield's most high-profile murder, that of 13-year-old Milly Dowler, police were able to place a car driven by him at the scene around the same time as Dowler's disappearance.

CAPTURE

Arrested in 2004 for the murder of French student Amélie Delagrange, Bellfield was later charged with the murder of Marsha McDonnell as well as several counts of rape, attempted murder, grievous bodily harm and assault. In 2010, Bellfield was charged with the kidnapping and murder of Milly Dowler.

SENTENCING

He received a life sentence for each of his three murder convictions.

**B. 1968
LOCATION: UK
YEARS ACTIVE:
2002–04
ALSO KNOWN AS:
"THE BUS STOP KILLER"
MURDERS: 3+**

HIROSHI MAEUE

Maeue had a paraphilia, or a sexual abnormality, that meant he could only attain sexual release by manual strangulation. He murdered three people, all of whom were members of an online suicide website, in a rented car.

MEANS

He used his bare hands to strangle his victims – nothing else could bring him to the same climax and temporary sexual fulfilment.

MOTIVE

Maeue told investigators that he thought his paraphilia was triggered as a child, when he read a mystery novel where a character was murdered in the same way. He said he was "sexually excited" by the sight of someone being suffocated and suffering.

OPPORTUNITY

Prior to the murders, he had previous form when it came to strangling people. He had attacked a friend at the Kanazawa Institute of Technology, where he was a student in the late 1980s. He was arrested for strangling a colleague in 1995, then two women in 2001. After being released from nearly two years in prison for strangling a schoolboy in 2002, he began lurking in the forums of an online suicide club. He approached three members of the club on separate occasions, offering to commit suicide with them by locking

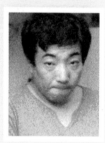

themselves in a car, burning charcoal and inhaling the smoke. A 14-year-old boy, a 21-year-old man and a 25-year-old woman met with him on three separate occasions, when he strangled them instead.

CAPTURE

When the body of 25-year-old Michiko Nagamoto was discovered in February 2005, buried in a riverbank in Kawachinagano, Osaka, police were able to trace her emails back to Maeue. When arrested in August, he admitted to the murder of two others by the same means.

SENTENCING

He was sentenced to death and executed by hanging on 28 July 2009.

**1968–2009
LOCATION: JAPAN
YEARS ACTIVE: 2005
MURDERS: 3**

INESSA TARVERDIYEVA

Tarverdiyeva was the mother in a middle-class family from Stavropol, who embarked on a series of brutal carjacking murders and home invasions with her husband Roman Podkopaev and two daughters, 25-year-old Viktoria and 13-year-old Anastasiya. They were known as "The Gang of Amazons".

MEANS

Tarverdiyeva used a semi-automatic Saiga carbine, a shotgun, pistols and a combat knife to kill. The family used a car as transport to and from the crime scenes.

MOTIVE

Cash, electronics, jewellery and other valuables were stolen from the victims, but considering the comfortable combined incomes of Tarverdiyeva and Podkopaev, a teacher and dentist respectively, the goods weren't their main aim. And the ferocity of the murders was shocking: two teenage girls who were ambushed in their own home had their eyes gouged out before they were shot. The crimes of the family have been compared to that of the Ma Barker Gang, with Tarverdiyeva taking the role of matriarch.

OPPORTUNITY

Tarverdiyeva and her husband would organize frequent "camping trips" with their daughters. The family would drive to their victim's houses or wait in the car and ambush their victims at the roadside.

CAPTURE

After a break-in on 8 September 2013 in the town of Aksay, a gunfight ensued in which Podkopaev and a police officer were killed. Tarverdiyeva and her daughters initially escaped but were arrested shortly after.

SENTENCING

Unbelievably, despite admitting to being a "gangster by nature" and showing no remorse, Tarverdiyeva was able to shift most of the responsibility for the murders onto her dead husband, and got a relatively light 21-year prison sentence.

**B.1967
LOCATION: RUSSIA
YEARS ACTIVE: 1998–2013
MURDERS: 30+**

FRANCISCA BALLESTEROS

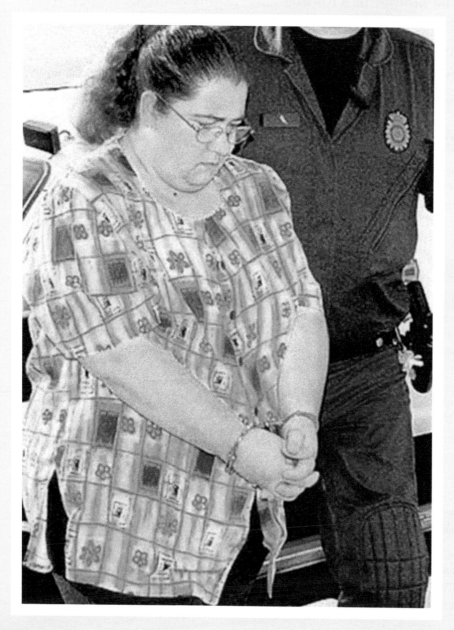

Ballesteros was a mother of three who murdered her husband, her two daughters and attempted to murder her son, in the Spanish city of Melilla, just off the north coast of Africa.

MEANS

She used high doses of prescription drugs to poison her victims: Colme, a medicine used to treat alcoholism, zolpidem and bromazepam, which are both sedatives. They were put in the victim's food or drink.

MOTIVE

After her first child Florinda was born, Ballesteros suffered from postnatal depression which could have easily contributed to the dark thoughts that led to her murdering five-month-old Florinda in 1990. After meeting a man online in 2004, she decided she needed to escape her current life by killing the rest of her family and fleeing back to her hometown of Valencia to be with him.

OPPORTUNITY

Her husband Antonio died of a fatal overdose of Colme, zolpidem and bromazepam in January 2004. Her daughter Sandra Ballesteros died of poisoning in June 2004 while her son, also called Antonio, survived being poisoned on the same day Sandra died.

CAPTURE

Hospital staff became suspicious after 12-year-old Antonio was admitted to hospital showing symptoms of poisoning. An autopsy of Sandra Ballesteros revealed the drugs in her system, and her mother was subsequently arrested.

SENTENCING

Ballesteros was sentenced to a total of 84 years in prison in 2005.

**B.1969
LOCATION: SPAIN
YEARS ACTIVE:
1990–2004
MURDERS: 3**

ZHOU KEHUA

Zhou Kehua was a robber who gave no thought to killing anyone who got in the way of him and the money.

MEANS

According to the Chinese authorities, Zhou was a hired gun for mercenary groups in Burma and owned a Type 54 pistol – even though private gun ownership is illegal in China. He had a history of serious crime, including convictions for illegal firearms and arms trafficking, for which he did time and "re-education through labour" in 1997 and 2004. At the time of his death, he was armed with two pistols, modified to be more powerful and house larger magazines.

MOTIVE

Profit appears to be Zhou's primary motive: he attacked people making cash deposits and withdrawals at the bank, shooting them in the head and looting them as they lay dead or dying.

OPPORTUNITY

Some of the 500,000 closed circuit television cameras deployed around Chongqing placed Zhou at the scene of the murders and robberies. He was recorded at Bank of China Savings Office in Shapingba District on 10 August 2012, four days before police cornered him. A cashier making a withdrawal was shot that morning, along with the two security guards who flanked her. These last killings are what sparked the manhunt for Zhou.

CAPTURE

DNA evidence and CCTV analysis allowed police to identify Zhou and trace his last movements. He was confronted in an alleyway, where he succumbed to two bullets after a short gunfight with the police.

**1970–2012
LOCATION: PEOPLE'S
REPUBLIC OF CHINA
DATES ACTIVE: 2004–12
MURDERS: 9+**

SONYA CALEFFI

Caleffi was a nurse who lived and worked in the far north of Italy, in the city of Como's Sant'Anna Hospital, and Lecco's Alessandro Manzoni Hospital. She murdered more than a dozen of her terminally ill patients in a relatively short period of time before she was discovered.

MEANS

She used a hypodermic syringe filled with nothing but air, enough to cause a fatal embolism (a blockage in the vein) when injected into a major blood vessel.

MOTIVE

Caleffi had suffered from poor mental health for years, dipping into bouts of depression and anorexia. In the year prior to her first known murders, she had attempted to commit suicide several times. But that moment when she held a syringe and someone else's fate in her hands was the only time she was in control – and the subsequent drama as the emergency team flocked to rescue the stricken patient made her feel alive. "I just wanted to draw attention to myself because I felt undervalued," she told the investigators in a letter, "... those people destined to die in a short time pitied me. That's why I accelerated the time of their death."

OPPORTUNITY

The patients in palliative care were in no condition to prevent her from injecting them, even if there was the slightest chance they knew exactly what she was doing.

CAPTURE

After multiple suspicious deaths were finally linked to Caleffi, she was arrested on 14 December 2004.

SENTENCING

Caleffi was given 20 years but was granted parole after 14 years for good behaviour, and released from Bollate prison on 25 October 2018.

**B.1970
LOCATION: ITALY
YEARS ACTIVE:
2003–2004
MURDERS: 15–18**

TODD CHRISTOPHER KOHLHEPP

The relatively smart and self-confident Kohlhepp was a South Carolina estate agent whose job allowed him to get his victims alone in empty properties.

MEANS

Kohlhepp had built up a successful real estate company in Moore, South Carolina, with a licence he had obtained despite being on the sex-offenders register for a serious crime he'd committed at age 15. He had bought a large tract of land, and as an estate agent, had the trust of strangers, whom he would take to empty properties and remote pieces of land.

MOTIVE

Kohlhepp had shown evidence of psychopathy as a child: he tortured small animals and had a furious temper, snapping when he didn't get his way. His first recorded sexual offence, which landed him on the sex-offenders register, was in 1986, when he kidnapped and raped a girl his own age at gunpoint, before walking her home and warning her not to tell anyone.

OPPORTUNITY

Kala Brown and her boyfriend Charles Carver disappeared after they went to clean Kohlhepp's house in 2016. Carver was shot dead immediately, while Brown was held in a soundproofed container on Kohlhepp's property for two months.

CAPTURE

The disappearance of Carver and Brown was immediately noticed. But strange posts that popped up on Facebook, and included Carver referring to himself in the third person – "kala is with her husband [sic] charlie" – prompted investigators to trace the couple's mobile phones to their last known location. When the police arrived at Kohlhepp's property, banging from inside the container alerted them to Brown's presence.

SENTENCING

Kohlhepp quickly confessed to murdering Charlie Carver, as well as a couple he had kidnapped under similar circumstances less than a year before, as well as the murders of four employees of a motorcycle store in a 13-year-old cold case. Apparently, Kohlhepp had snapped after they had refused him a refund and allegedly laughed at his inability to ride the bike he had purchased. He got a life sentence for each of the seven murders.

**B. 1971
LOCATION: USA
YEARS ACTIVE: 2003–16
MURDERS: 7**

ANDRZEJ NOWOCIEŃ

Nowocień was a paramedic at the centre of racket at a hospital in Łódź, central Poland. He murdered elderly patients in order to pass their details onto a local undertaker and receive a cut of the fee the deceased family was charged. He and his accomplices were known as the "skin hunters", after they referred to the bodies of the victims as "skins".

MEANS

The patients were injected with a muscle relaxant, Pavulon, in the ambulance on the way to the hospital. In their critical condition, death would quickly follow.

MOTIVE

Nowocień could receive a month's wages or more in a single bribe from the undertakers. In a slow month of "skin hunting", hastening the death of someone who was likely to die soon anyway proved too tempting a prospect.

OPPORTUNITY

With his fellow paramedic Karol Banaś and two doctors, Dr Janusz Kuliński and Dr Paweł Wasilewski, also taking bribes, it was a simple case of administering the drug en route in the privacy of the ambulance and having a doctor friendly to his cause sign the death certificate.

CAPTURE

Investigative reporters from Polish newspaper *Gazeta Wyborcza* discovered that Łódź hospital staff were taking bribes from local funeral homes. Nowocień was arrested in 2002 along with the three others implicated in the crimes.

SENTENCING

Nowocień was convicted of four murders and given a life sentence. He later boasted of killing many more patients to another prison inmate.

**B.(EXACT AGE UNKNOWN) 1967
LOCATION: POLAND
YEARS ACTIVE: 1990
(SUSPECTED)–2002
MURDERS: 4+**

SERGEI DOVZHENKO

This former soldier and policeman apparently snapped in 1998 and, over the course of three years, murdered at least 17 people in Mariupol, southeast Ukraine.

MEANS

Dovzhenko used a variety of weapons to dispatch his victims, including a pistol and a knife. He wore his old police uniform and produced a fake police ID badge on at least one occasion to gain his victims' trust.

MOTIVE

He claimed to almost exclusively seek revenge on those who "mocked him" and those who had "stolen his future": the recruiting police officers who refused to employ Dovzhenko following their suspicions that he had been involved in the 1998 murder of security guard Sergei Mitchenko. By committing these murders, he hoped to tank the police department's credibility in solving them and thus humiliate those who had refused to let him on the force. He also murdered to remove any living witnesses to the money he stole in some of the murder cases.

OPPORTUNITY

Many of his apparently random victims were killed after advertising valuables for sale in the local newspapers: Lyudmila Shevchenko and her son Sergei were murdered after advertising a video camera in September 1999. Ivan Vakulenko and his son Vitaly were murdered in December 1999 after trying to sell a computer. Galina Ivanova and her granddaughter Tanya were murdered in an elaborate effort to distract the police from the murder of their neighbour, Claudia Bondarenko, who had begun to suspect that Dovzhenko, a friend of her son, was behind the recent spate of murders.

CAPTURE

Following another double murder in May 2002, Dovzhenko was arrested.

SENTENCING

Dovzhenko was sentenced to life imprisonment in September 2003.

**B.1972
LOCATION: UKRAINE
YEARS ACTIVE: 1998–2002
MURDERS: 17+**

ALEXANDER PICHUSHKIN

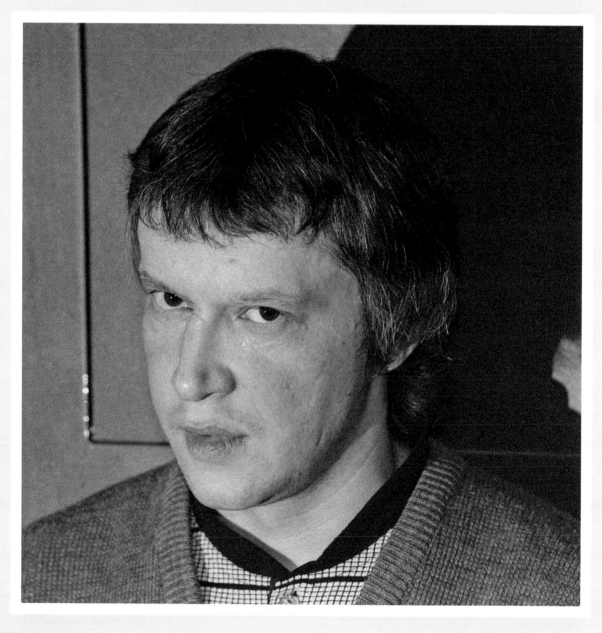

Pichushkin is one of Russia's worst serial killers, murdering most of his victims in Moscow's Bitsa Park. He played chess with 20 of the people he killed.

MEANS

He engaged some of his victims in a game of chess and sedated them with strong alcohol, before striking them with a hammer. He used an empty vodka bottle and sticks to penetrate their skulls. Their bodies were roughly buried in the park or thrown into the sewer that ran through the park. He filled the squares of a chessboard in his flat to keep a record of his kills.

MOTIVE

Pichushkin was hit in the head by a swing when he was a child, after which his behaviour was observed to have changed. He became increasingly aggressive and impulsive as he got older, culminating in these premeditated bouts of extreme violence. "I liked the sound of a skull splitting," he told prosecutors, explaining, "For me, life without killing is like life without food for you. I felt like the father of all these people, since it was I who opened the door for them to another world."

OPPORTUNITY

Many of Pichushkin's murders were of homeless men easily lured away to quieter parts of the park with the promise of alcohol. His final known victim was 36-year-old Marina Moskalyova, who worked in the same shop as Pichushkin. She was murdered in Bitsa Park as she walked home with him in June 2006.

CAPTURE

After a metro ticket with a date and time stamp was discovered on Moskalyova's body, police checked CCTV footage at the station she exited from and spotted Pichushkin accompanying her. He was arrested that same month.

SENTENCING

In 2007, he was convicted of 49 murders and three attempted murders, and given a life sentence.

**B.1974
LOCATION: RUSSIA
ALSO KNOWN AS: "THE
CHESSBOARD KILLER"
YEARS ACTIVE:
1992–2006
MURDERS: 49+**

STEPHEN PORT

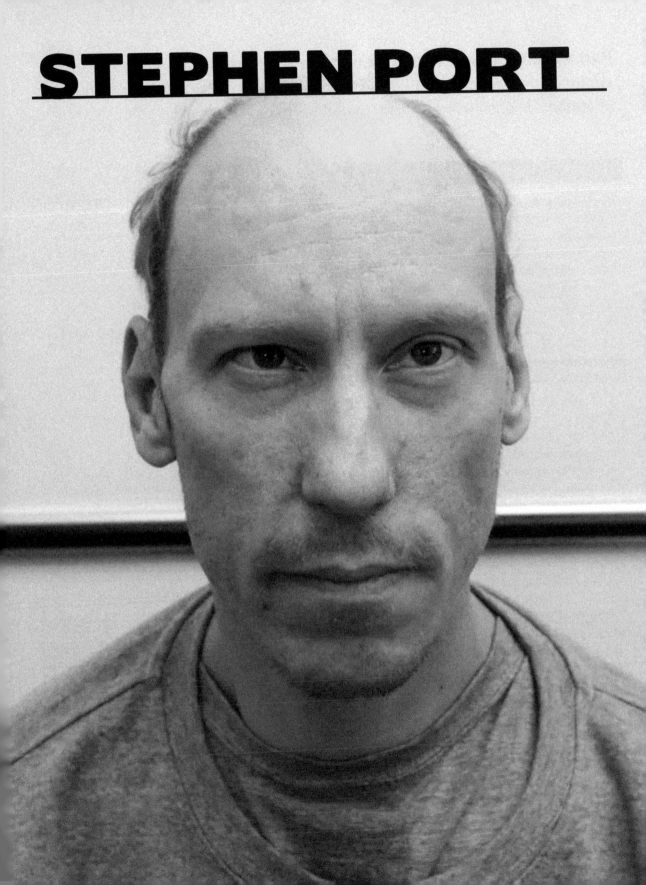

Port was a rapist and murderer who lived in South East England and whose victims were mainly men in their twenties, some of whom he was in contact with on social networks and dating apps such as Grindr.

MEANS

He used alcohol laced with an illegal substance known as GHB (a known date-rape drug) to render his victims unconscious. His four known victims died from the strong doses he administered without their knowledge. He also left a fake suicide note on the body of one of his victims, Daniel Whitworth.

MOTIVE

Port knew that he could have consensual sex with each of his victims before he drugged them, but in each case he wanted to fulfil a rape fantasy. He had no issue with spiking the drinks he prepared for them with fatal doses of GHB, as long as it kept them unconscious long enough for him to satisfy himself.

OPPORTUNITY

Two of his known victims, Daniel Whitworth and Jack Taylor, he met on the gay dating app Grindr. Anthony Walgate was an escort and Gabriel Kovari was an old housemate of Port's. He arranged a meeting in the flesh with each, before taking them back to his east London flat, where they were offered a drink. Port would then surreptitiously prepare the tainted beverage in another room. Their bodies were dumped in a nearby graveyard.

CAPTURE

Police were able to trace Jack Taylor's last known movements and see him accompanying Port back to his flat. Port was already known to the police in connection with Anthony Walgate's death, and he was arrested in October 2015.

SENTENCING

He was convicted of four murders in November 2016, although he is suspected to have killed many more. He was given a life term without the possibility of parole.

**B.1975
LOCATION: UK
YEARS ACTIVE:
2014–2015
MURDERS: 4+**

BEATE ZSCHÄPE

Zschäpe was a member of a neo-Nazi terrorist group, who was convicted of the murders of 10 people in seven different cities across Germany. She was the only surviving member to be prosecuted, after Uwe Mundlos and Uwe Böhnhardt chose to commit suicide before they could be caught.

MEANS

Each of the murder victims was shot with a silenced CZ 83 pistol. Two attempts at murder were made with homemade pipe bombs in Cologne and the city district of Cologne-Mülheim, but no loss of life resulted.

MOTIVE

The murders were mainly politically and racially motivated. Eight of the victims were of Turkish origin and one was Greek. A German police officer was also murdered.

OPPORTUNITY

Each of the victims was shot in cold blood, usually at their place of work. Two bullets killed 49-year-old Abdurrahim Özüdoğru in a tailor's shop, 38-year-old Enver Şimşek was murdered inside his flower shop van, and 31-year-old Süleyman Taşköprü was shot three times in his greengrocer's shop.

CAPTURE

Zschäpe handed herself in to police on 8 November 2011, four days after Mundlos and Böhnhardt committed suicide.

SENTENCING

She was sentenced to life imprisonment without parole on 11 July 2018.

B.1975
LOCATION: GERMANY
YEARS ACTIVE: 2000–2011
MURDERS: 10

NICOLA SAPONE

Sapone was the ringleader of a satanic cult known as the "Beasts of Satan", who masterminded the ritualistic murders of three people in Northern Italy. He was suspected of many more murders.

MEANS

Assisted by Andrea Volpe, Marco Maccione and several others, Sapone's first two victims were stabbed with knives and beaten with a hammer, and his final victim was shot with a pistol then beaten to death with a shovel. Shovels were used to bury the bodies of all three of their known victims.

MOTIVE

Some blamed the death metal music the group enjoyed for encouraging Sapone and the Beasts of Satan to engage in extreme acts of violence. But what drove Sapone to kill is certain to be more complicated than that: a combination of anti-social personality disorders and a knee-jerk reaction to Italy's traditional Catholic values undoubtedly played a big role in his motivation to murder.

OPPORTUNITY

The victims were all known to Sapone. Nineteen-year-old Chiara Marino and 16-year-old Fabio Tollis, who were friends with Marco Maccione, disappeared after a night out at the Midnight Pub in the town of Somma Lombardo in January 1998. Twenty-seven-year-old Mariangela Pezzotta was Volpe's ex-girlfriend; he invited her over to dinner with the intention of killing her, because Sapone thought she had too much information about the Beasts of Satan.

CAPTURE

When Volpe attempted to get rid of Pezzotta's car by driving it into a nearby river, he crashed it instead, and the police wanted to know what he was doing in possession of her vehicle. Volpe eventually confessed to the murders, leading to the arrest of Sapone in 2005.

SENTENCING

He was convicted of three murders and sentenced to life imprisonment in 2006.

**B.1976
LOCATION: ITALY
YEARS ACTIVE: 1998–2004
MURDERS: 3+**

173

WILLIAM HOLBERT

American-born Holbert was responsible for the murders of five US citizens in the Bocas del Toro archipelago, on the east coast of Panama.

MEANS

He used a gun to shoot his victims dead and the remote cover of the jungle to bury their bodies. He turned the house he stole from three of his victims, the Brown family, into a party pad to attract more ex-pats. Blood was found on Holbert's boat, which was used to transport the bodies.

MOTIVE

Profit was Holbert's only motive. He stole real estate and property from his victims, claiming that they had left the area and sold it to him cheaply.

OPPORTUNITY

The former Brown home became known as "The Jolly Roger Social Club" by Holbert's neighbours. It was here that he would encounter two more US ex-pats who became his victims: 58-year-old Bo Icelar and 53-year-old Cheryl Hughes.

CAPTURE

Friends and neighbours became suspicious when Cheryl Hughes suddenly went missing and Holbert claimed her home. After the police made the journey to the island, Holbert and his wife fled. They were arrested over the border in Nicaragua.

SENTENCING

He was convicted of five murders in 2017 and sentenced to 47 years in a Panamanian prison.

**B.1979
LOCATION: PANAMA
YEARS ACTIVE:
2007–2010
MURDERS: 5**

RAMADAN MANSOUR

Mansour was a gang leader who murdered children and adolescents between Cairo and Alexandria. He was nicknamed "Al-Tourbini", or "Express Train", by fellow gang members because of his favourite killing method.

MEANS

He would lure children, mostly boys, off the street and onto the roof of the express train from Cairo to Alexandria. Here he would rape and torture his victims before throwing them off the roof of the moving train, which would usually finish them off if they weren't dead already. He felt more comfortable killing away from Cairo because there were fewer police, which partly explains his odd means of murder.

MOTIVE

He confessed to the police that rape was a way of exacting revenge on those he felt had wronged him, though he also told prosecutors that he was possessed by a female jinn (an evil spirit).

OPPORTUNITY

It was relatively easy for Mansour, a man who had himself lived on the streets from an early age, to convince street children to join him on the roof of a train. One of his murder victims was a young member of his gang who had reported him to the police for raping him. Mansour was released on this occasion due to lack of evidence.

CAPTURE

Police had a file on Mansour for some time before his final arrest in 2007, along with his accomplice Farag Samir Mahmoud.

SENTENCING

Mansour was sentenced to death and executed in 2010.

**1980–2010
LOCATION: EGYPT
YEARS ACTIVE:
1999–2007 (ESTIMATED)
MURDERS: 32+**

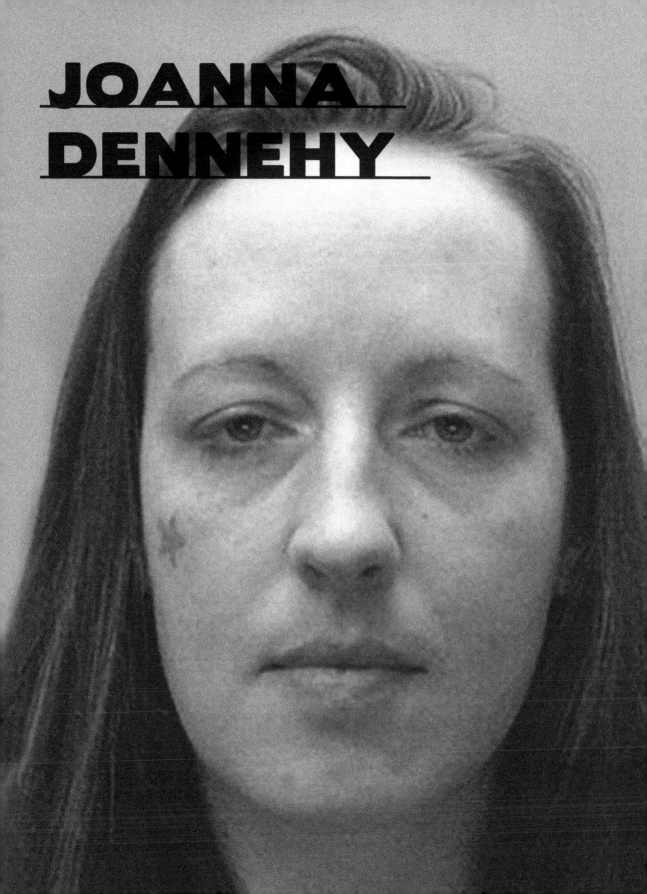

JOANNA
DENNEHY

Joanna Dennehy is responsible for the "Peterborough ditch murders", killing three men over a short period of time in South East England.

MEANS

All three of Dennehy's victims were stabbed to death in frenzied attacks. Amid her spree, a photograph of her licking the tip of a vicious "zombie" knife popped up on social media, suggesting her cold-blooded intentions. She routinely kept a dagger in one of her boots and told friends in the lead-up to her crimes that she felt like killing someone. She could not have been as effective a killer without her two accomplices, Gary Stretch and Leslie Layton, who helped her locate victims and dispose of the bodies.

MOTIVE

A year prior to the three murders, Dennehy spent a few days being psychologically assessed in Peterborough City Hospital; doctors diagnosed her with a psychopathic, anti-social personality disorder. She also derived sexual pleasure from inflicting pain on herself and others, and Dennehy admitted to acquiring a taste for murder after her first kill.

OPPORTUNITY

Her murder victims were either former lovers or men who had annoyed Dennehy with the attention they lavished on her. Lukasz Slaboszewski was keen to become romantically involved with Dennehy, John Chapman was her housemate, and Kevin Lee was her landlord, boss and lover. The two men who survived being stabbed by Dennehy were chosen at random after she left the house with Stretch to "get my fun".

CAPTURE

She was arrested in April 2013 and pleaded guilty in November the same year.

SENTENCING

Dennehy was sentenced to life imprisonment, with no possibility of parole.

**B. 1982
LOCATION: UK
DATES ACTIVE:
19–29 MARCH 2013
MURDERS: 3**

DAVID MULCAHY

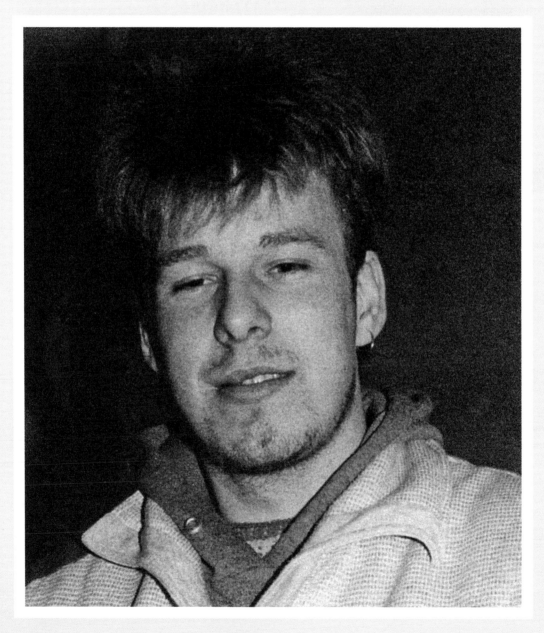

Over the course of a year in the mid-1980s, Mulcahy murdered several women and raped many more in the south of England, along with his accomplice and close friend John Duffy.

MEANS

He used rocks or blunt instruments to bludgeon their victims, then ligatures to strangle them. These were fashioned from a type of twine that Duffy had access to or in one case, the murder of Maartje Tamboezer, from a stick and the Dutch schoolgirl's own belt. The pair would listen to Michael Jackson's song "Thriller" while making preparations for the next attack.

MOTIVE

Mulcahy first found pleasure in inflicting pain on animals, then later escalated to humans – first rapes, then murders. Author Simon Farquhar, the son of the detective who handled the case, said he didn't consider Mulcahy a typical serial killer because the murders weren't compulsive – they were "recreational" and just a hobby to Mulcahy.

OPPORTUNITY

With Duffy's help, Mulcahy targeted lone women at quiet stations along a stretch of railway line just outside London. They worked in tandem, ambushing victims or setting traps, like the length of fishing line they stretched across the road to force Maartje Tamboezer off her bicycle. They referred to this as "hunting", a chilling reminder that these crimes were a game to them.

CAPTURE

Duffy was captured and imprisoned in 1988, but lack of evidence meant Mulcahy was free until 2000, when Duffy finally testified against him.

SENTENCING

Mulcahy was convicted of three murders and seven rapes, and received three life sentences.

**B.1959
LOCATION: UK
YEARS ACTIVE:
1985–1986
MURDERS: 3**

DELLEN
MILLARD

Millard was the playboy son of a millionaire aviation business owner. He killed three people in cold blood in the Toronto area, including his own father.

MEANS

He used pistols in two of the murders: a Walther PPK to kill Tim Bosma and a .32-calibre Smith & Wesson to kill his father. The remains of his ex-girlfriend Laura Babcock were never discovered, though she was also shot. Millard and his accomplice, Mark Smich, disposed of Tim Bosma's body in a large agricultural incinerator.

MOTIVE

Millard was a narcissist who believed he was above the rules and that he was entitled to whatever he desired. His father Wayne Millard was murdered to expedite Dellen's inheritance, while Millard killed Laura Babcock to please his new girlfriend, who was jealous of her. Tim Bosma was shot dead in order to steal his pickup truck – for the thrill of it, rather than financial gain.

OPPORTUNITY

His most infamous murder was that of Tim Bosma, who was selling his 2007 Dodge Ram pickup truck on an auto-trading website when Millard responded to the advert. Millard and Smich arrived at the Bosma residence to give the vehicle a test drive. Bosma went with them, and never returned.

CAPTURE

Millard was eventually identified by a distinctive "ambition" tattoo on his wrist, which had been described by the owners of another pickup truck Millard had test-driven prior to Tim Bosma's murder. He was arrested in May 2013.

SENTENCING

He was given life imprisonment without the possibility of parole for 25 years.

**B.1985
LOCATION: CANADA
YEARS ACTIVE:
2012–2013
MURDERS: 3**

IGOR SUPRUNYUK

Over the course of three weeks, Suprunyuk and his accomplice Viktor Sayenko bludgeoned nearly two dozen people to death in cold-blooded attacks that shocked the city of Dnipropetrovsk, central Ukraine. They were known as the "Hammer Maniacs".

MEANS

Suprunyuk used a hammer or steel bar to strike his victims and beat them to death. He would sometimes hold his weapon discreetly in a plastic bag to disguise it from a prospective target. He also used a screwdriver or blade to stab them. Both youngsters used mobile phones to take photos and videos of their victims as they tortured and murdered them.

MOTIVE

Long before either of them became serial killers, Suprunyuk suggested that they "overcome their fears" by dangling from the fourteenth floor of their family home. He also encouraged them to overcome their "squeamishness" by torturing and murdering small animals. Both teenagers had effectively desensitized themselves to the escalation of violence they were about to embark on and Suprunyuk, at least, was displaying hallmarks of psychopathology in his eagerness to murder people. The detective who worked the case stated simply that they thought they both were "doing it as a hobby, to have a collection of memories when they get old".

OPPORTUNITY

A pregnant woman, two young teenagers, a sick man, drunks and elderly people: there was no pattern to the murders other than they were relatively easy targets and that they had the misfortune to be passing by Suprunyuk and Sayenko as they lay in wait, often in woods outside the city.

CAPTURE

On 23 July 2007, when Suprunyuk tried to sell a mobile phone he stole from one of his victims to a pawnshop and the shop owner turned it on, police were able to trace the signal to the shop. Using descriptions of the killers provided by witnesses to two of the murders, police identified Suprunyuk and Sayenko, and arrested them.

SENTENCING

Suprunyuk tried to make an insanity plea, but the court did not accept it. He was found guilty of 21 murders and given a life sentence.

B.1988
LOCATION: UKRAINE
YEARS ACTIVE: 2007
MURDERS: 21

PAVEL VOITOV

As the leader of a gang of bloodthirsty neo-Nazis, Voitov organized and participated in a series of horrific murders in Moscow. The gang members mainly targeted homeless people and called themselves "cleaners".

MEANS

Each of Voitov's victims was stabbed with a combat, lock or craft knife. Some were also beaten with a hammer.

MOTIVE

Voitov and his gang members were part of an extreme far-right community who abhorred alcoholics and sought to "clean the city" of homeless people.

OPPORTUNITY

The times and places of the murders were chosen to minimize the chance of Voitov and his gang's crimes being witnessed. Victims were attacked in parks, abandoned buildings, under bridges and in areas away from CCTV cameras. They struck in the dead of night, between the hours of 1am and 4am. There was one survivor: a janitor that Voitov and another gang member attacked at Vykhino metro station, who managed to fend them off.

CAPTURE

After the unsuccessful murder attempt at Vykhino, the surviving janitor was able to provide a description of his attackers to Moscow police and the FSB, Russia's federal security agency. Voitov was arrested in February 2015.

SENTENCING

In October 2017, Voitov was given a life sentence.

B.1994
LOCATION: RUSSIA
YEARS ACTIVE: 2014–2015
MURDERS: 14+

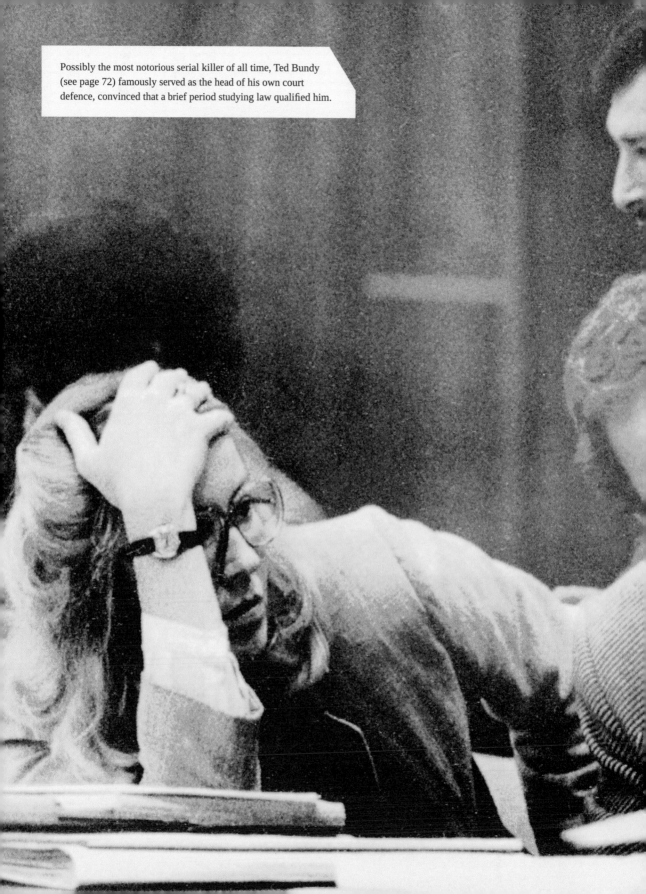

Possibly the most notorious serial killer of all time, Ted Bundy (see page 72) famously served as the head of his own court defence, convinced that a brief period studying law qualified him.

INDEX

CREDITS